Teach Yourself

VISUALLY™

Windows® XP
Special Media Edition

by Sherry Willard Kinkoph

Visual™

From

maranGraphics®

&

WILEY

Wiley Publishing, Inc.

Teach Yourself VISUALLY™
Special Media Edition

Published by
Wiley Publishing, Inc.
111 River Street
Hoboken, NJ 07030-5774

Published simultaneously in Canada

Library of Congress Control Number: 2004103157

ISBN: 0-7645-5716-5

Manufactured in the United States of America

10 9 8 7 6 5 4 3 2 1

1K/RX/QT/QU/IN

Trademark Acknowledgments

Important Numbers

For U.S. corporate orders, please call maranGraphics at 800-469-6616 or fax 905-890-9434.

For general information on our other products and services or to obtain technical support please contact our Customer Care Department within the U.S. at 800-762-2974, outside the U.S. at 317-572-3993 or fax 317-572-4002.

Permissions

Wiley Publishing, Inc.

U.S. Corporate Sales
Contact maranGraphics at (800) 469-6616 or fax (905) 890-9434.

U.S. Trade Sales
Contact Wiley at (800) 762-2974 or fax (317) 572-4002.

Some comments from our readers...

"I have to praise you and your company on the fine products you turn out. I have twelve of the *Teach Yourself VISUALLY* and *Simplified* books in my house. They were instrumental in helping me pass a difficult computer course. Thank you for creating books that are easy to follow."

– *Gordon Justin (Brielle, NJ)*

"I commend your efforts and your success. I teach in an outreach program for the Dr. Eugene Clark Library in Lockhart, TX. Your *Teach Yourself VISUALLY* books are incredible, and I use them in my computer classes. All my students love them!"

– *Michele Schalin (Lockhart, TX)*

"Like a lot of other people, I understand things best when I see them visually. Your books really make learning easy and life more fun."

– *John T. Frey (Cadillac, MI)*

"I have quite a few of your Visual books and have been very pleased with all of them. I love the way the lessons are presented!"

– *Mary Jane Newman (Yorba Linda, CA)*

"I write to extend my thanks and appreciation for your books. They are clear, easy to follow, and straight to the point. Keep up the good work!"

– *Seward Kollie (Dakar, Senegal)*

"I am an avid fan of your Visual books. If I need to learn anything, I just buy one of your books and learn the topic in no time. Wonders! I have even trained my friends to give me Visual books as gifts."

– *Illona Bergstrom (Aventura, FL)*

"Thank you for making it so clear. I appreciate it. I will buy many more Visual books."

– *J.P. Sangdong (North York, Ontario, Canada)*

"I was introduced to maranGraphics about four years ago and YOU ARE THE GREATEST THING THAT EVER HAPPENED TO INTRODUCTORY COMPUTER BOOKS!"

– *Glenn Nettleton (Huntsville, AL)*

"Compliments to the chef!! Your books are extraordinary! Or, simply put, extra-ordinary, meaning way above the rest! THANK YOU THANK YOU THANK YOU! for creating these."

– *Christine J. Manfrin (Castle Rock, CO)*

"I just purchased my third Visual book (my first two are dog-eared now!) and, once again, your product has surpassed my expectations. The expertise, thought, and effort that go into each book are obvious, and I sincerely appreciate your efforts. Keep up the wonderful work!"

– *Tracey Moore (Memphis, TN)*

"Thank you, thank you, thank you...for making it so easy for me to break into this high-tech world. I now own four of your books. I recommend them to anyone who is a beginner like myself. Now...if you could just do one for programming VCR's, it would make my day!"

– *Gay O'Donnell (Calgary, Alberta, Canada)*

"You're marvelous! I am greatly in your debt."

– *Patrick Baird (Lacey, WA)*

Dec '02

maranGraphics is a family-run business
located near Toronto, Canada.

At **maranGraphics**, we believe in producing great computer books — one book at a time.

maranGraphics has been producing high-technology products for over 25 years, which enables us to offer the computer book community a unique communication process.

Our computer books use an integrated communication process, which is very different from the approach used in other computer books. Each spread is, in essence, a flow chart — the text and screen shots are totally incorporated into the layout of the spread.

Introductory text and helpful tips complete the learning experience.

maranGraphics' approach encourages the left and right sides of the brain to work together — resulting in faster orientation and greater memory retention.

Above all, we are very proud of the handcrafted nature of our books. Our carefully-chosen writers are experts in their fields, and spend countless hours researching and organizing the content for each topic. Our artists rebuild every screen shot to provide the best

clarity possible, making our screen shots the most precise and easiest to read in the industry. We strive for perfection, and believe that the time spent handcrafting each element results in the best computer books money can buy.

Thank you for purchasing this book. We hope you enjoy it!

Sincerely,

Robert Maran
President
maranGraphics
Rob@maran.com
www.maran.com

CREDITS

Project Editor
Timothy J. Borek

Acquisitions Editor
Jody Lefevere

Product Development Manager
Lindsay Sandman

Copy Editor
Marylouise Wiack

Technical Editor
Dennis R. Short

Editorial Manager
Robyn Siesky

Manufacturing
Allan Conley
Linda Cook
Paul Gilchrist
Jennifer Guynn

Illustrators
Karl Brandt
Ronda David-Burroughs
David E. Gregory
Sean Johanessen
Steven Schaerer

Book Design
maranGraphics®

Production Coordinator
Maridee Ennis

Layout
Sean Decker
LeAndra Hosier
Kristin McMullan
Heather Pope

Screen Artist
Jill A. Proll

Proofreader
Susan Sims

Quality Control
John Greenough
Susan Moritz

Indexer
Tom Dinse

**Vice President and
Executive Group Publisher**
Richard Swadley

Vice President and Publisher
Barry Pruett

Composition Director
Debbie Stailey

ABOUT THE AUTHOR

Sherry Willard Kinkoph has written over 50 books over the last 9 years covering a variety of computer topics ranging from hardware to software, from Microsoft Office programs to the Internet. Her recent titles include *Teach Yourself VISUALLY Flash 5, Master VISUALLY Dreamweaver MX and Flash MX,* and *Microsoft Office 2003: Top 100 Simplified Tips & Tricks.* Sherry's ongoing quest is to help users of all levels master the ever-changing computer technologies. No matter how many times they — the software manufacturers and hardware conglomerates — throw out a new version or upgrade, Sherry vows to be there to make sense of it all and help computer users get the most out of their machines.

AUTHOR'S ACKNOWLEDGMENTS

Special thanks go out to acquisitions editor, Jody Lefevere, for handing me such a fun book to tackle; to project editor, Tim Borek, for shepherding the book from start to finish, never missing a beat; to copy editor, Marylouise Wiack, for ensuring that all the i's were dotted and t's were crossed; to technical editor, Dennis Short, for checking everything over for accuracy and offering his skilled observations; and finally to the production team at Wiley for their efforts in creating such a visual masterpiece.

To my husband, Greg, for always encouraging
me and sharing a passion for computer
gadgets and software.

TABLE OF CONTENTS

Chapter 1

GETTING STARTED WITH WINDOWS XP MULTIMEDIA

Chapter 2

WORKING WITH DIGITAL CAMERAS AND SCANNERS IN WINDOWS XP

Chapter 3

WORKING WITH IMAGES IN THE MY PICTURES FOLDER

Chapter 4

Chapter 5

Chapter 6

TABLE OF CONTENTS

Chapter 7

PLAYING AUDIO FILES WITH WINDOWS MEDIA PLAYER

Chapter 8

PLAYING MUSIC FROM THE MY MUSIC FOLDER

Chapter 9

DOWNLOADING AND RECORDING AUDIO FILES

Chapter 10

LISTENING TO INTERNET RADIO

Chapter 11

PLAYING DVDS WITH WINDOWS MEDIA PLAYER

TABLE OF CONTENTS

Chapter 14

ADDING EXTRA EFFECTS TO VIDEO CLIPS IN WINDOWS MOVIE MAKER

Chapter 15

DOWNLOADING AND RECORDING VIDEO FILES

Chapter 16

PLAYING WINDOWS XP GAMES

CHAPTER 1

Getting Started with Windows XP Multimedia

Windows XP offers a variety of rich multimedia features. In this chapter, you learn all the basics about multimedia and how to use image, audio, and video files with Windows XP.

INTRODUCTION TO WINDOWS XP MULTIMEDIA FEATURES

Windows XP offers a variety of multimedia features. You can quickly tap into features, such as listening to audio CDs, downloading music from the Internet, viewing and editing videos and photos, and burning music CDs.

Windows XP comes in two versions: Windows XP Home Edition and Windows XP Professional Edition. The Home Edition includes features that are for home and small business use. The Professional Edition offers more features for business users. You can use this book to learn about multimedia elements found in each edition.

Defining Multimedia

The term *multimedia* encompasses everything from graphics to music and videos to computer games. Windows XP is designed to handle multimedia applications and large multimedia files more efficiently than previous versions of Windows.

Viewing Images

You can use the My Pictures folder along with the Windows Picture and Fax viewer to view images that you upload from your digital camera, download from the Web, or scan in using a scanning device. Chapter 2 shows you how to make Windows XP work with digital cameras and scanners. Chapters 3 and 5 show you various ways to view your stored images.

Using Images with Windows XP

You can turn your favorite photograph into a wallpaper image that appears on your computer's desktop, or even into a screen saver. Windows XP also includes features that allow you to create a photo album, e-mail images, and publish images on the Web. Chapter 4 shows you how to get the most out of your stored images.

Working with Music and Sound

Windows XP installs with a program called Windows Media Player, which enables you to play tracks from an audio CD, burn tracks to a new CD, create a playlist, and download music from the Internet. Chapters 6 to 8 show you how to use the Windows Media Player program and the My Music folder to play and organize audio files. Chapter 9 explains how to download and record audio files. Chapter 10 shows you how to listen to Internet radio stations.

Working with Video Footage

Windows Movie Maker allows you to copy video footage from a digital camcorder and make simple edits to create your own movies. For example, you can trim a video clip and add your own title text and audio effects. Chapters 11 to 15 show you how to work with video files.

Playing Games

Games combine graphics, sound, and animation to create interactive play. Windows XP installs with several simple games, such as Spider Solitaire, FreeCell, and Pinball. When you tire of playing computer games on your own, you can go online and play with multiple users. Chapter 16 shows you how to get the most out of your Windows XP games.

TYPES OF MULTIMEDIA FILES

Windows XP allows you to work with a variety of multimedia file types. By recognizing a multimedia file, you can determine which Windows XP feature you can use to view the file.

Windows XP displays icons in front of the filenames to help you recognize the file type in a folder. You can also identify file types by their *extension,* the three-letter suffix following the filename. By default, Windows XP does not display file extensions.

Graphic Files

Graphic files are typically artwork that you create on a computer. For example, when you create artwork in a drawing program, such as Windows Paint, you save it as a graphic file. Clip art — pre-drawn artwork that installs with some programs — is also stored as a graphic file type. Graphic file types include GIF and BMP formats. You can view graphics in the My Pictures folder or with the Windows Picture and Fax Viewer.

Image Files

Image files can include pictures that you take with a digital camera or upload from a scanner. You can save image files as a variety of graphic file types, including the JPG, BMP, TIF, and PNG file formats. You can view image files in the My Pictures folder or using the Windows Picture and Fax Viewer.

Audio Files

Audio files include music and other sounds that have been turned into digital formats, or *digitized*. Audio files come in a variety of file types. Native to Windows, the WAV file type is a popular format for sound clips, such as special effects that you can add to a movie or a slide show presentation. MP3, WMA, and MIDI are popular formats for music files, such as music you download from the Web. You can listen to audio files using Windows Media Player.

Video Files

Using Windows Media Player, you can view video information that you download from the Web, such as movie trailers and music videos. You can also use Windows Movie Maker, a video-editing program that comes with Windows XP, to view clips and edit footage that you record and download to your computer. AVI, MPEG, MOV, and WMV are popular video file formats that are recognized by Windows XP.

VIEW FILE EXTENSIONS IN WINDOWS XP

By default, Windows XP does not display file extensions. You can choose to display file extensions in any Windows XP folder to help you recognize multimedia file types so that you can quickly determine what type of data a file contains.

File extensions are the letters that follow the filename, and are preceded by a period. File extensions can range from one letter to five letters and identify the type of data stored within the file. For example, .bmp identifies a bitmap graphic file and .mp3 identifies a sound file.

VIEW FILE EXTENSIONS IN WINDOWS XP

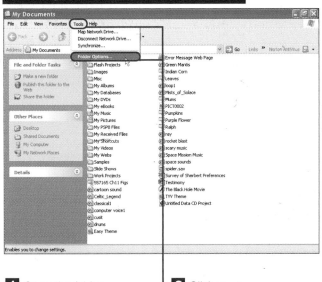

1 Open the folder containing the multimedia files you want to view.

2 Click **Tools**.

3 Click **Folder Options**.

■ The Folder Options dialog box appears.

4 Click the **View** tab.

5 Click **Hide file extensions for known file types** (☑ changes to ☐).

■ You can use the scroll arrows to scroll through the options list to find the check box you want to deselect.

Can I turn the file extensions off again?

Yes. Repeat the steps shown below, but click the **Hide file extensions for known file types** check box in the Folder Options dialog box to activate the feature and hide the file extensions again.

How can I learn which file types can be viewed on my computer?

You can click the **File Types** tab in the Folder Options dialog box to view a complete list of all the file types registered to work with your computer system. You can also use this tab to change which program opens a file type when you select the file. For example, you may prefer to play a movie file in Internet Explorer rather than Windows Media Player. To change the associated program, click the file type, click the **Change** button, and then select another program from the list that appears.

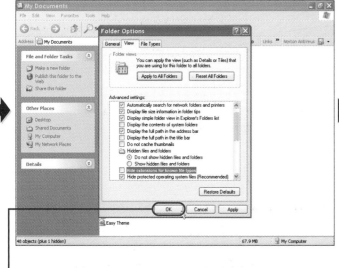

6 Click **OK**.

■ The Folder Options dialog box closes.

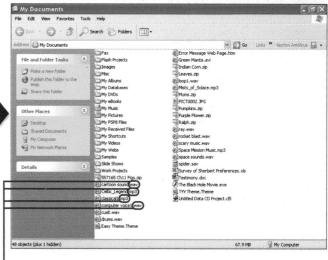

■ The file extensions display in the filenames.

UNDERSTANDING DIGITAL IMAGES

Before you begin working with graphics, photos, and other image files in Windows XP, it is a good idea to learn about how image files work with your computer. This can help you to edit and manage your files more effectively.

Pixels

Digital images, whether graphics, photos, or clip art, are comprised of pixels. The word *pixel* stands for *picture element*. A pixel appears as a tiny square on your screen, and is the basic building block of any digital image that you view on your computer. Pixels are arranged vertically and horizontally, much like a grid, to create an image.

Resolution

The number of pixels in an image determines the resolution, or clarity, of the image. The more pixels an image uses, the higher the image resolution. Higher resolutions result in more picture details. If an image uses fewer pixels, then the overall image appears unclear, and the edges appear jagged.

High
Quality

Low
Quality

PPI and DPI

Pixel resolution is measured in pixels per inch, or *PPI*. PPI are similar to *DPI*, or dots per inch, a measurement for printer quality. The main difference between the two is that pixels are square and dots are round. Most computer screens can display resolutions of 72 or more PPI.

Bit Depth

Bit depth is the number of possible colors in a palette or color spectrum that are used to create an image. Common color bit depths include 8-bit color, which produces a palette of 256 colors, 16-bit color, which produces a palette of 65,536 colors, and 24-bit color, which produces 16 million colors.

Data Compression

To help reduce file sizes, image file formats use different types of data compression. *Lossy* compression works by losing portions of redundant or unnecessary image data without creating a very noticeable difference in overall image quality. *Lossless* compression can reduce file size by 10 to 50 percent — depending on the file format in which you save your image — and results in less image degradation.

Choosing Image File Formats

As you work with various image files and image-editing programs on your computer, you can choose a file format that best suits the way in which you want to use the file. The JPEG file format, one of the most popular image formats used today, uses lossy compression, an efficient data compression that allows you to create a much smaller file size than that of a lossless format. This makes the JPEG format better suited for photographic image files. BMP, TIF, and PNG file formats use lossless compression, which does not compress data as much as the JPEG format, but works well for simple graphics and logos.

UNDERSTANDING DIGITAL AUDIO

When you listen to and work with different types of sound files on your computer, it helps to know how digital audio works in Windows XP. Understanding basic concepts behind audio files can help you edit and manage the files on your computer more effectively.

Analog and Digital

Before the advent of computers, music and sound was recorded in analog format. Analog sound recordings are continuous representations of changes in the sound or air pressure captured by a microphone. Digital recordings create digital representations of sound by measuring values in discrete intervals. You can store digital sounds on a computer and play them back using a player program, such as Windows Media Player, or a portable player device.

Digital Sounds

Although sounds are invisible, they are made up of waves that vary in size, or time, and volume. For computer usage, sounds are transformed into mathematical equations called *digital sampling*. The size of a digital sample is measured in bits. Unlike analog, digital audio can create an exact copy of a sound, and subsequent digital copies recreate the sound without losing sound quality. Digital quality is measured by how many samples exist in a single second of the sound, called the *sampling rate*.

Digital File Formats

There are a variety of popular audio file formats that you can use with Windows XP. To determine which format you should use, you must first decide how you plan to use the audio file. For short sound effects that you want to use in another file, such as a slide presentation, the WAV format works well. WAV files are uncompressed. For music files that you want to listen to using a player, such as Windows Media Player, MP3 and WMA are the most popular choices, especially for music you download from the Web or burn onto an audio CD. Other audio formats include QuickTime, or AIFF, and RealAudio, or RA.

MP3 Files

MP3 is one of the Moving Picture Experts Group, or MPEG, file formats, and first emerged as a technology for file compression. MP3 compression works by removing extra sounds captured by the recording session that are not noticeable by human ears, making the audio files one-tenth the size of normal audio files. The smaller file size makes MP3 files easy to download from the Internet. Portable MP3 players are widely available; allowing you to create your own song mixes and to listen to music while you are traveling.

WMA

Windows Media Audio, or WMA, is another format for encoding digital audio files. The latest codec, Windows Media 9 Professional, offers good audio quality and a smaller file size. The WMA format works similarly to MP3, but can compress files at a compression rate of up to 20 percent more than MP3. This allows you to store more music files on a portable player device.

Copyrights and Licenses

Now that digital audio files are so easy to copy and share, the technology poses a threat to copyrighted works. To ensure that your music files are legal, you can use digital licenses. A digital license links an audio file to a particular person or computer, much like a software license links a copy of a software program to you and the computer on which you store and use it. You can also subscribe to online pay-for-play services that allow you to download audio files for a fee.

UNDERSTANDING DIGITAL VIDEO

You can use Windows XP to store and view video clips and content from DVDs on your computer. Digital video format is a high-quality imaging format that refers to video signals stored in a digital format. Understanding a few basic digital video concepts can help you to better manage and edit your video files.

Analog versus Digital

Prior to the introduction of digital media equipment, video content was viewed and stored in analog format. Motion picture films and VHS cassette tapes are two examples of analog media. Today's digital video formats offer higher-quality imaging. You cannot use analog content on your computer without first digitizing it.

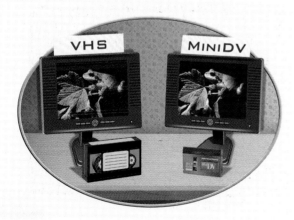

Record Digital Media

One way to digitize video is to shoot it with a digital camcorder. MiniDV camcorders record the highest-quality digital images, followed by Digital 8, or D8, camcorders. If your camcorder has i.LINK or FireWire output and your computer has an IEEE 1394 port, then you can transfer the video footage directly to a video-editing program on your computer.

IEEE 1394

IEEE 1394 is a standard for transferring digital information between peripheral devices, such as a DV camcorder, and your computer. The standard is also referred to by the trade names *FireWire,* by Apple Computer, or *i.LINK,* by Sony Corporation. With an IEEE 1394 cable and port, you can also control your camcorder directly from within a video-editing program, such as Windows Movie Maker 2.

Editing Requirements

Digital video consumes a great deal of disk space. To store one hour of digital video on a computer hard drive, you need 12.9 gigabytes, or GB, of free space. Keep this in mind when storing video clips on your computer. Large-capacity, high-speed hard drives work best for digital video editing.

Digitizing Analog Media

If you use an analog camcorder, such as 8mm or Hi8, then you can turn analog footage into digitized video using a video capture device. Many types of analog capture cards that install in your computer help you convert analog video from various sources, including VHS tapes.

Digital Video File Formats

Windows Media Video, or WMV, is a format that you can use in both Windows Media Player and Windows Movie Maker, two programs that come with Windows XP. Windows Media Player also lets you view AVI and MPEG formats. To view QuickTime and Flash movies, you require a separate player program.

STORE MULTIMEDIA FILES

You can store your multimedia files in folders that you create in Windows XP, or you can use the default folders. The My Documents folder includes three multimedia folders to help you organize different types of multimedia files on your computer.

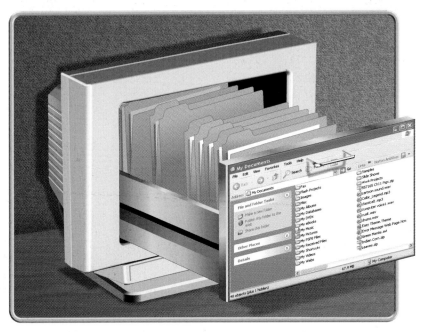

You can create numerous subfolders in each multimedia folder to create even more levels of organization for your files.

My Pictures

You can use the My Pictures folder to store your digital images and graphic files in one easy-to-find location. The folder includes extra image-related task links in the Task pane to help you work with image files.

My Music

You can use the My Music folder to store your digital music files and sound clips. The folder includes a few audio-related task links in the Task pane to help you work with music and sound files.

My Videos

You can use the My Videos folder to store digital video clips. Like the other two specialized folders, the My Videos folder also contains a few video-related task links to assist you in viewing and managing video files.

You can search for a particular multimedia file from within any folder in Windows XP. For example, if you open the My Documents folder, then you can search for a picture, a music file, or a video using the Windows XP search tools.

SEARCH FOR MULTIMEDIA FILES

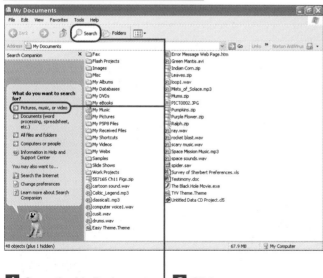

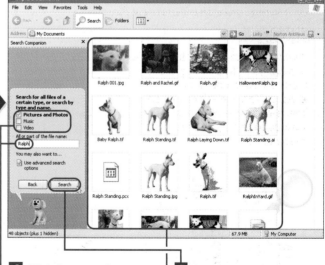

1 Open the My Documents folder or any multimedia folder window.

2 Click **Search**.

3 Click **Pictures, music, or video**.

4 Click the type of multimedia file that you want to locate (☐ changes to ☑).

5 Type all or part of the file name.

6 Click **Search**.

■ Windows XP searches for the file and displays any matches in the list area of the window.

CHAPTER 2

Working with Digital Cameras and Scanners in Windows XP

If you are setting up your digital camera or scanner to work with Windows XP, then this chapter can show you some practical ways to import images from these two sources.

With Windows XP's new image-management features, you can easily capture images from digital cameras and scanners and store them on your computer. Windows XP automatically recognizes most devices that you connect to your computer and immediately installs the drivers needed to help the devices communicate with your computer.

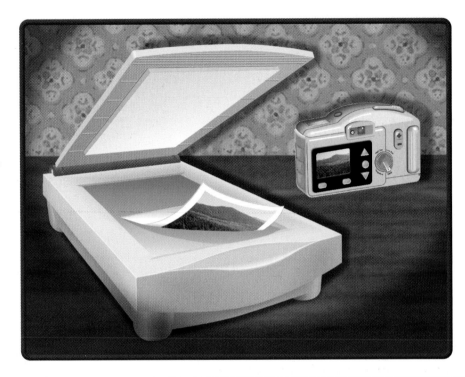

About Digital Cameras

Digital cameras record images using *pixels*. Depending on your camera, each picture you take contains 1 to 5 megapixels, or millions of pixels. Professional digital SLR cameras can shoot 10 megapixels and upward. With most digital cameras on the market today, captured images are stored on media cards, also called memory cards. Depending on the camera, some media cards are removable. Media cards come in different storage sizes, from 16MB to 256MB and more. The bigger the card capacity, the more photos you can take with the camera.

From the Camera to Your Computer

When you connect a digital camera or memory card reader to a computer running Windows XP, Windows immediately attempts to recognize the device. You rarely need to install driver files. When Windows XP recognizes the device, it treats the device as a disk drive, enabling you to view, copy, and move any images it contains.

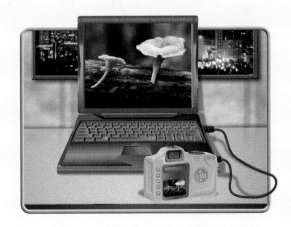

Scanners

You can acquire photographic prints using a scanner. A scanner acts much like a copier that sends your photo to your computer instead of to a sheet of paper. You can then store the digitized photo as a file on your computer, from which you can send it via e-mail or edit it in an image-editing program.

Digital Image Terminology

When you download pictures from a digital camera, the process is referred to as *acquiring*. When you scan an image, Windows XP identifies the action as a *scan event*. When you connect a digital camera for downloading images, Windows XP identifies the action as a *connect event*.

WIA Standard

Using the WIA standard, which stands for Windows Image Acquisition, you can integrate imaging devices, such as digital cameras and scanners, and work directly with images before you download them to your computer. For example, you can use the Open dialog box in any application to view the contents of your digital camera. Windows XP views the device much like an additional storage area or hard drive.

CONFIGURE A DIGITAL CAMERA OR SCANNER

With Windows XP, installing and configuring a digital camera or scanner is easier than ever before. You can tell the Scanner and Camera Installation Wizard exactly which manufacturer made your device and which model you are using. You can also instruct Windows XP to launch a particular editing program when encountering new images.

Agfa
Casio
Epson
Hewlett Packard
Dell

CONFIGURE A DIGITAL CAMERA OR SCANNER

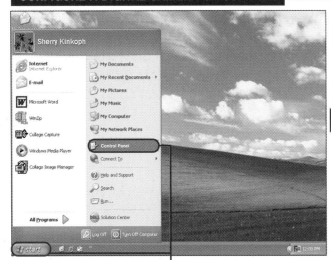

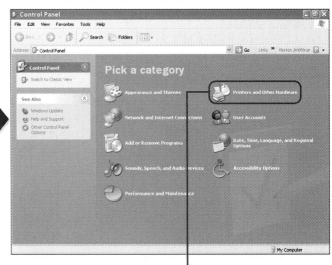

Note: Be sure to connect the digital camera or scanner to your computer and turn it on first before attempting to configure the device.

1 Plug the device into the appropriate port and turn on the digital camera or scanner.

2 Click **start**.

3 Click **Control Panel**.

■ The Control Panel window appears.

4 Click **Printers and Other Hardware**.

I see a pop-up notification. Do I still need to use the Scanner and Camera Installation Wizard?

No. When you plug in a device, Windows XP may detect it immediately and display a Found New Hardware message. You do not need to activate the Scanner and Camera Installation Wizard if you see this pop-up notification.

Found New Hardware

How do I remove a device I no longer use?

The Scanners and Cameras window lists all the devices you install as scanners and digital cameras. To remove a device you no longer use, right-click the icon for the device and click **Delete**. Windows XP removes it from the list.

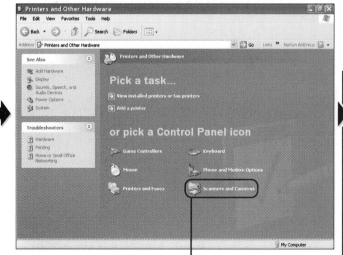

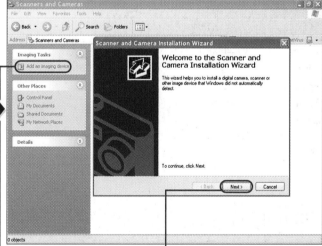

■ The Printers and Other Hardware window appears.

5 Click **Scanners and Cameras**.

■ The Scanners and Cameras window appears.

6 Click **Add an imaging device**.

■ The Scanner and Camera Installation Wizard appears.

7 Click **Next**.

CONTINUED

CONFIGURE A DIGITAL CAMERA OR SCANNER

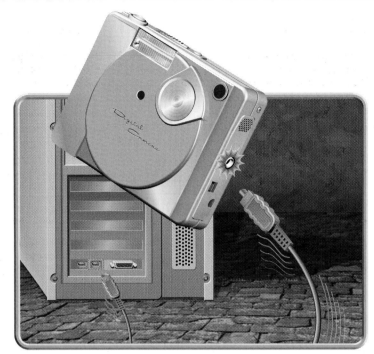

In the process of installing and configuring a digital camera or scanner, you can specify which port you want to use to help Windows XP recognize the device. The easiest method is to tell Windows XP to look for the connected device with the Automatic Detection option. You can also assign a distinct name to the device to help you easily recognize it on your computer.

After configuring a camera or scanner, the Scanners and Cameras window in the Control panel lists an icon for the device.

CONFIGURE A DIGITAL CAMERA OR SCANNER (CONTINUED)

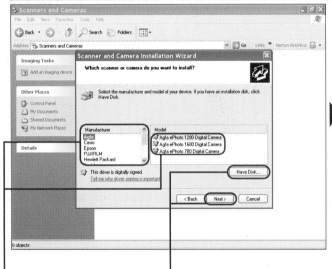

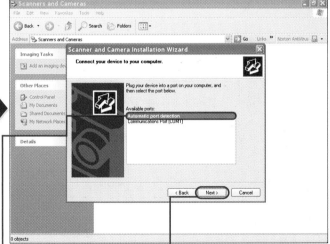

■8 Scroll through the list of manufacturers and select the manufacturer name for your camera or scanner.

■9 Click the device model.

■ If your camera or scanner came with a disk, then you can insert the disk, click the **Have Disk** button, and install the drivers for the device.

■10 Click **Next**.

■ The port selection page appears.

■11 Click **Automatic port detection**.

■ If you know which port you are using to connect the device, then you can select the port from the list.

■12 Click **Next**.

I installed my digital camera, but when I open the Scanners and Cameras window again, it is not listed. Why not?

Be sure to turn the device on first and then open the Scanners and Cameras window. Windows does not display an icon for the device unless the camera is plugged in and turned on.

I do not see my digital camera or scanner manufacturer or model listed in the Wizard. What should I do?

Try installing the device using Windows XP Device Manager instead. To open Device Manager, click **start**, and then click **Control Panel** to open the Control Panel window. Click the **Performance and Maintenance** link, and then click **System**. The System Properties dialog box appears. On the **Hardware** tab, click **Device Manager**. The Device Manager window appears. To learn more about installing a device this way, click the **Action** menu and select **Help**.

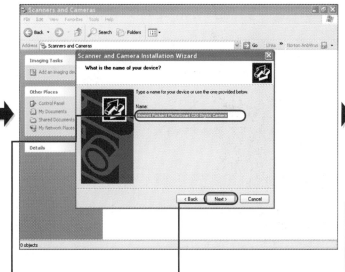

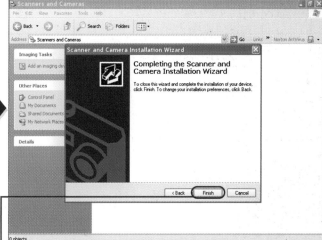

■ The device identification page appears.

13 Type a descriptive name for the device.

■ You can also use the default name that the Wizard assigns.

Note: The name you enter here appears in Windows Explorer, so be sure to clearly describe the device so that you can recognize it again later.

14 Click **Next**.

■ The completion page appears.

15 Click **Finish**.

■ The Scanner and Camera Wizard completes the installation, and the new device is listed in the Scanners and Cameras window.

UPLOAD PICTURES FROM A DIGITAL CAMERA

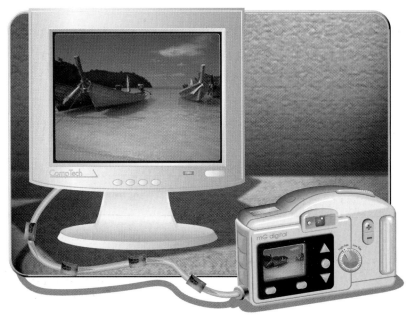

You can upload pictures from a digital camera to your computer without using any proprietary software that came with the camera. You can use the Scanner and Camera Wizard to select which photos you want to upload, as well as delete images that you no longer want to store on your camera's storage card.

If you use a card reader device, then you can use these same steps to upload images from the memory or media card without needing to plug in your camera.

UPLOAD PICTURES FROM A DIGITAL CAMERA

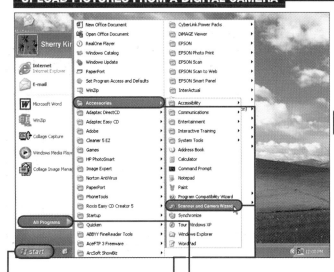

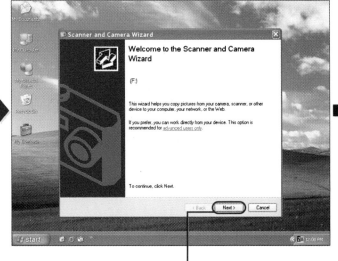

1 Plug in your camera or digital storage card reader.

Note: You may need to turn the camera on and activate a mode switch before uploading pictures.

2 Click **start**.

3 Click **All Programs**.

4 Click **Accessories**.

5 Click **Scanner and Camera Wizard**.

Note: The Scanner and Camera Wizard does not work with all digital cameras.

■ The Scanner and Camera Wizard appears.

6 Click **Next**.

I cannot open the Scanner and Camera Wizard. Why not?

Depending on how you set up the software, you may still be able to use the Scanner and Camera Wizard. When you plug in your camera or card reader, a prompt like the one shown here may appear, asking what action you want to perform. One of the options in the list is to use the Microsoft Scanner and Camera Wizard. You can make your selection from the list of options and click **OK**.

■ A new page appears, displaying thumbnails of your pictures.

7 Select the check box next to any pictures that you want to upload (☐ changes to ☑).

■ You can click a check mark to deselect a picture you do not want to upload (☑ changes to ☐).

■ To rotate a picture, click the picture and click a rotation button.

8 Click **Next**.

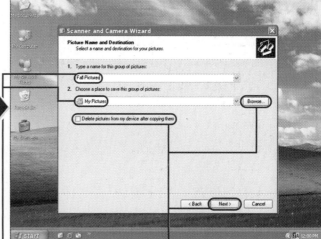

■ The Picture Name and Destination page appears.

9 Type a name for your group of pictures.

10 Click ☑ to designate a folder to save the pictures to, or leave the default folder selected.

■ You can click **Browse** to navigate to another folder.

■ If you want to delete the pictures from your camera or memory card after uploading, then click this option (☐ changes to ☑).

11 Click **Next**.

CONTINUED ▶

UPLOAD PICTURES FROM A DIGITAL CAMERA

By default, Windows XP stores your uploaded pictures in the My Pictures folder, unless you specify another folder. Depending on your computer and the number of pictures you captured on the camera, the uploading process may take a few seconds or several minutes. After you finish the uploading procedure, you can view your pictures in the folder you selected.

UPLOAD PICTURES FROM A DIGITAL CAMERA (CONTINUED)

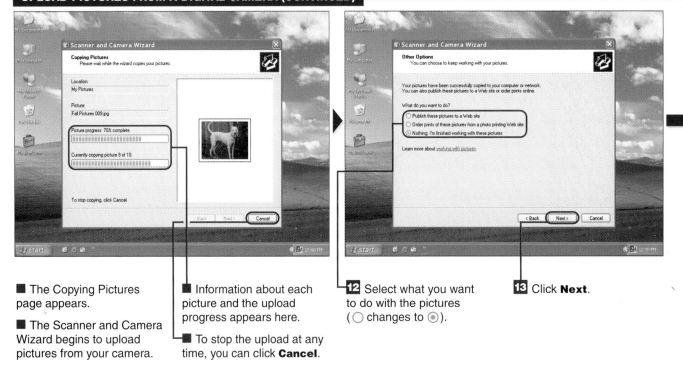

■ The Copying Pictures page appears.

■ The Scanner and Camera Wizard begins to upload pictures from your camera.

■ Information about each picture and the upload progress appears here.

■ To stop the upload at any time, you can click **Cancel**.

12 Select what you want to do with the pictures (○ changes to ◉).

13 Click **Next**.

Does the Scanner and Camera Wizard name each of my photos after uploading?

The Scanner and Camera Wizard assigns a common filename to your uploaded pictures, based on the group name you enter. For example, if you typed Vacation as your group name, then the Wizard names all the pictures you upload with the filename Vacation, followed by individual picture numbers, such as Vacation 001 and Vacation 002.

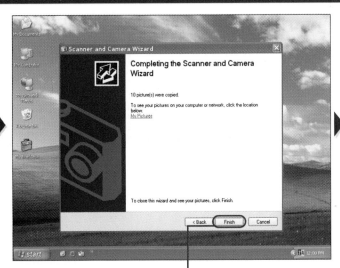

■ The Wizard completion page appears.

14 Click **Finish**.

■ The Scanner and Camera Wizard window closes.

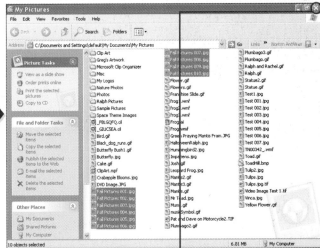

■ The My Pictures folder window appears automatically and highlights the newly uploaded pictures.

Note: See Chapter 3 to learn more about viewing images in the My Pictures folder.

15 Click ⊠.

■ The My Pictures folder window closes.

COPY PICTURES FROM A DIGITAL CAMERA TO A CD

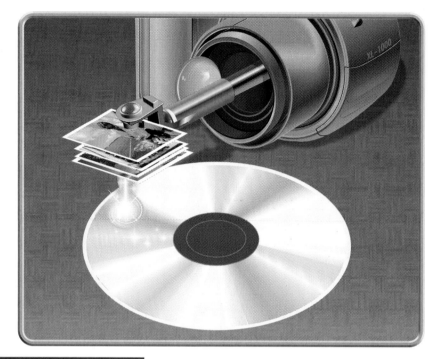

You can copy pictures from your camera to a recordable CD. Windows XP offers some basic picture management functions that you can use to work with pictures directly in your camera or digital card reader device without uploading the pictures to your hard disk drive.

COPY PICTURES FROM A DIGITAL CAMERA TO A CD

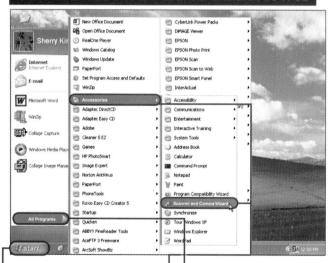

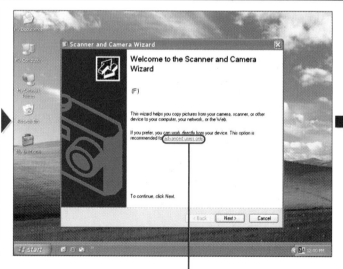

1 Plug in your camera or memory card reader.

Note: You may need to turn the camera on and activate a mode switch before uploading pictures.

2 Click **start**.

3 Click **All Programs**.

4 Click **Accessories**.

5 Click **Scanner and Camera Wizard**.

Note: The Scanner and Camera Wizard does not work with all digital cameras.

■ The Scanner and Camera Wizard appears.

6 Click **advanced users only**.

Do I have to use the Scanner and Camera Wizard to access my camera's pictures?

No. You can access pictures directly if Windows XP lists your camera or card reader in My Computer. You can open the My Documents folder window and navigate to the device using the Address bar ⌄.

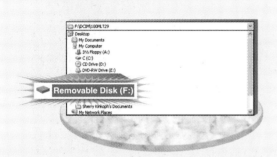

What other file management features can I perform on my pictures?

You can copy, move, and rename your pictures as well as perform other file management tasks in the folder window. For example, you can e-mail a picture, turn it into a desktop background, or create a photo album. To learn more about working with pictures, see Chapters 3, 4, and 5.

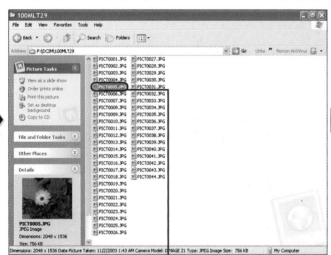

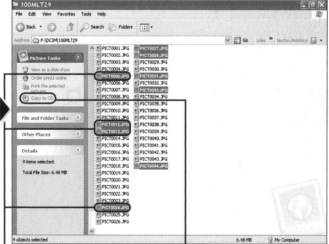

■ A folder window appears, displaying the camera or card reader's contents.

■ You may need to double-click the folder name to list the camera's pictures, or open more than one folder to navigate to the pictures list.

■ To preview a picture, click the picture filename.

7 Select the pictures you want to copy.

■ To select multiple pictures, you can press and hold the **Ctrl** key while clicking pictures you want.

8 Click the **Copy to CD** link in the task pane.

CONTINUED ▶

COPY PICTURES FROM A DIGITAL CAMERA TO A CD

You can choose to copy all of your pictures to a CD, or select only certain pictures to copy. After you copy the pictures, you can use the same folder window to navigate to the CD and view the copied images.

COPY PICTURES FROM A DIGITAL CAMERA TO A CD (CONTINUED)

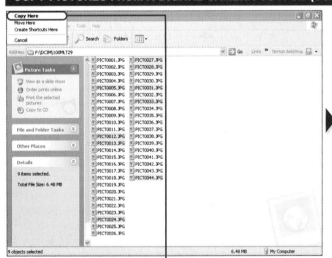

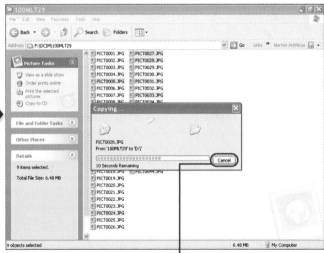

■ A pop-up menu appears.

9 Insert a blank, recordable CD in your computer's CD-ROM drive.

10 Click **Copy Here**.

■ Windows XP copies the pictures to the CD.

■ Depending on the number of pictures you selected and the speed of your computer, the copying process may take a few seconds or several minutes.

■ If you need to cancel the copying process, then you can click **Cancel**.

Can I print my pictures directly from the camera?

Yes. You can select the pictures you want to print, then activate the Print this picture or Print the selected pictures link under the Picture Tasks heading in the folder window's task pane. The Photo Printing Wizard immediately appears, and guides you through the steps for printing photos. To learn more about printing pictures and ordering online prints, see Chapter 3.

Can I copy pictures from my computer to my camera's media card?

Yes. If you have room on the media or memory card, then you can transfer pictures from your computer to the card. You can do this as a way to share pictures if a friend or family member's camera also accepts the same type of media card.

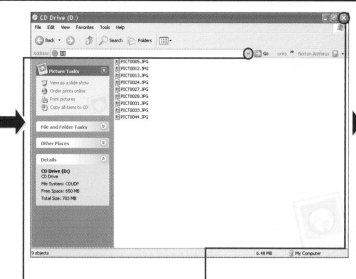

■ You can click ⌄ to navigate to the CD-ROM drive to view the copied pictures.

11 Click ✕ when you finish copying the pictures.

■ The folder window closes.

12 Click **Cancel** to close the Scanner and Camera Wizard.

DELETE PICTURES FROM A DIGITAL CAMERA

Windows XP allows you to delete pictures you no longer want from your camera or media card. You can erase pictures from your camera to free up storage for new pictures later on.

To make sure you do not remove a picture you want to keep, you should first upload your pictures onto your computer's hard drive. Not all cameras allow you to work directly with the camera's pictures through the folder window. You may have to use the software that came with the camera to delete those pictures.

DELETE PICTURES FROM A DIGITAL CAMERA

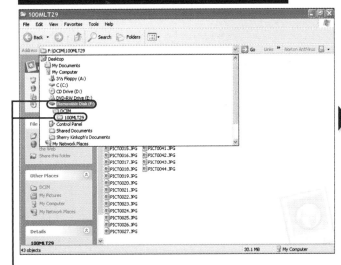

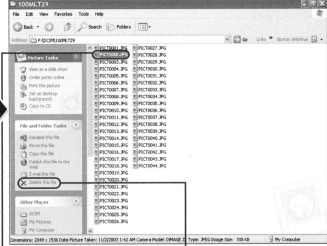

1 Open the folder for your camera or card reader device in the My Documents window.

Note: You can also use the Scanner and Camera Wizard to work directly with your camera. See the previous section, "Copy Pictures from a Digital Camera to a CD," for more information.

2 Select the picture or pictures that you want to delete.

■ To select multiple pictures for deletion, press and hold the **Ctrl** key while clicking picture filenames.

3 Click the **Delete this file** link.

Can I remove pictures with the Scanner and Camera Wizard?

Yes. As you progress through the steps of uploading your pictures, the Picture Name and Destination page in the Scanner and Camera Wizard offers an option for deleting pictures from the device after uploading. By default, this check box is deselected, so if you do want to delete pictures, be sure to check this box before proceeding with your upload. After the Wizard uploads the pictures, it removes them from the camera or media card.

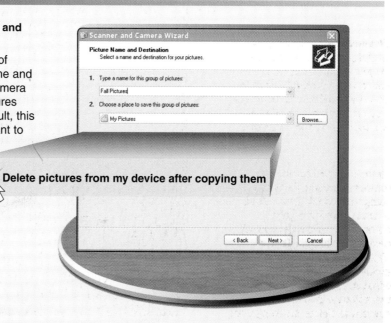

Delete pictures from my device after copying them

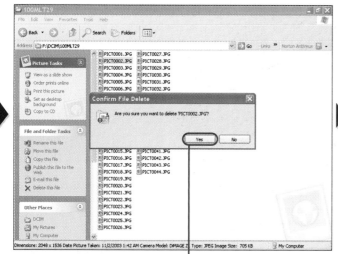

■ The Confirm File Delete dialog box appears.

4 Click **Yes**.

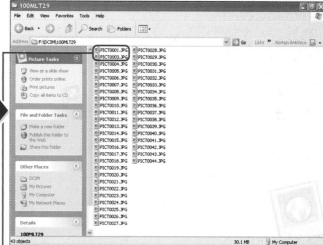

■ Windows XP permanently removes the picture file or files from the camera or media card.

SCAN A PICTURE

You can scan a picture using a scanner and store it on your computer. For example, you can scan a photo to use in a document or to publish later on a Web page. Scanning is one way that you can import digital images to your computer. You can use the Scanner and Camera Wizard to guide you through the scanning procedure.

SCAN A PICTURE

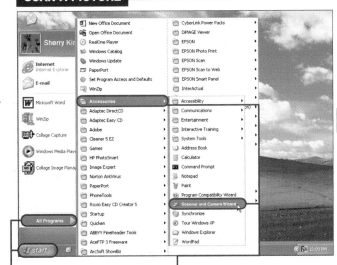

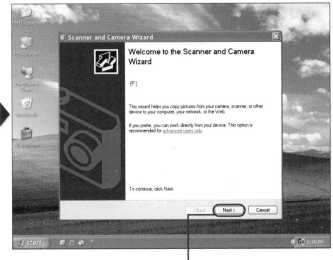

1 Turn on your scanner and position a photo on the scanner bed.

2 Click **start**.

3 Click **All Programs**.

4 Click **Accessories**.

5 Click **Scanner and Camera Wizard**.

Note: The Scanner and Camera Wizard does not work with all scanners.

■ The Scanner and Camera Wizard appears.

6 Click **Next**.

How do I crop an image in the Scanner and Camera Wizard?

In the Choose Scanning Preferences page in the Wizard, click the **Preview** button to create a preview of the scan. Drag the handles around the image preview if you want to crop your picture to a smaller size. For example, you may want to crop out the edges of a picture so the subject matter receives more attention.

I cannot activate the Scanner and Camera Wizard. Why not?

Make sure your scanner is connected properly to your computer and is turned on. See the section "Configure a Digital Camera or Scanner" to enable Windows XP to work with your scanner. The Scanner and Camera Wizard does not support all scanners. If your scanning device does not support the WIA standard, then you must use the proprietary software that comes with the scanner in order to operate the device.

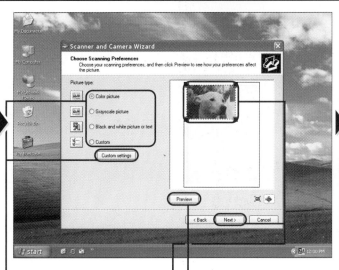

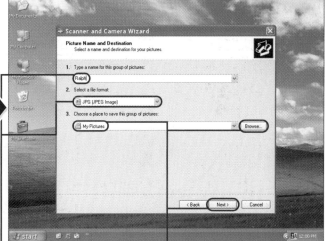

■ The scanning preferences page appears.

7 Click the picture type that you want to scan (○ changes to ⊙).

■ You can click **Custom settings** to set additional scan options.

8 Click **Preview**.

■ A preview of the scanned image appears here.

■ If you do not like the preview image, then you can adjust the picture in the scanner before proceeding with the actual scan.

9 Click **Next**.

■ The Picture Name and Destination page appears.

10 Type a name for the image.

11 Select a file format for the image.

Note: The Scanner and Camera Wizard supports the JPEG, BMP, TIF, and PNG file formats, with JPEG often as the default selection.

12 Select a destination folder for the scan.

■ You can click **Browse** and select another folder.

13 Click **Next**.

SCAN A PICTURE

After you scan a picture, you can specify how you want to work with the image. You can view your newly scanned image in the default My Pictures folder window, or in the folder you designated when determining where to save the picture file.

SCAN A PICTURE (CONTINUED)

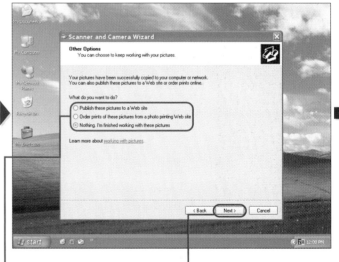

■ The Scanning Picture page appears.

■ The Scanner and Camera Wizard begins scanning the picture.

■ This area displays information about the scan's progress.

■ You can click **Cancel** to stop the scan procedure.

■ The Other Options page appears.

14 Select what you want to do with the scanned image (○ changes to ◉).

15 Click **Next**.

How do I view a picture I have previously scanned?

If you store your scanned pictures in the My Pictures folder or in a subfolder within the default folder, you can use the folder window to preview and manage your scanned picture files. See Chapter 3, 4, and 5 to learn more about working with picture files in Windows XP and using the My Pictures folder window to manage your images.

I do not like my scanned picture results. How do I redo the scan?

You can delete the file from the My Pictures folder window and activate the Scanner and Camera Wizard again to rescan the image. You can click the **Custom settings** button in the second Wizard page to open a Properties dialog box and adjust the brightness, contrast, and resolution settings for the scan.

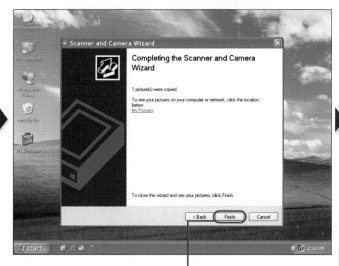

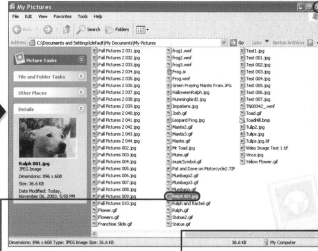

■ The completion page appears.

16 Click **Finish**.

■ The Scanner and Camera Wizard closes.

■ The folder window appears, displaying the newly scanned image.

■ The scanned picture's filename appears highlighted in the list view.

17 Click ✕ to close the window when you are finished viewing the picture.

My Pictures

CHAPTER 3

Working with Images in the My Pictures Folder

Are you ready to view your digital photographs? You can use the My Pictures folder as your central base for working with digital images you store on your computer. This chapter shows you how you can store, view, and print your snapshots, all from within the My Pictures folder.

OPEN THE MY PICTURES FOLDER

To help you quickly access your digital photos, Windows XP automatically creates a handy storage folder called My Pictures inside the default My Documents folder. The My Pictures folder not only stores your digital images in one easy-to-remember location but also includes links to common tasks for working with your images.

You can create subfolders within the My Pictures folder to further organize images you store on your computer. For example, you can create a folder for family snapshots and another folder for vacation pictures.

OPEN THE MY PICTURES FOLDER

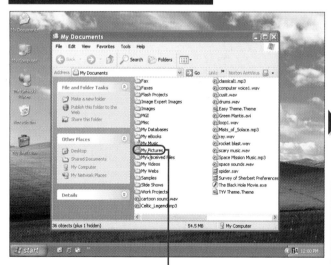

1 Open the My Documents or My Computer window.

■ You can double-click the My Documents folder on the desktop or click **Start** and then **My Documents**.

2 Double-click **My Pictures**.

■ The My Pictures folder window appears.

■ A list of links to common tasks appears in the left pane of the folder window.

■ To close the folder window at any time, click ☒.

NAVIGATE THE MY PICTURES FOLDER

You can keep track of your digital images using the My Pictures folder. The folder window includes a toolbar for navigating folders on your computer as well as a pane containing links to common commands.

Menu Bar

Displays menus which, when clicked, reveal commands for managing your files and folders.

Standard Buttons

Displays shortcut buttons to common tasks, such as navigating between folders and changing folder views.

Title Bar

Displays the name of the open folder.

Address Bar

You can go directly to a folder and file if you type the path in this bar and click the **Go** button.

Task Pane

The left side of the folder window lists links to common tasks, folders, and details about your files.

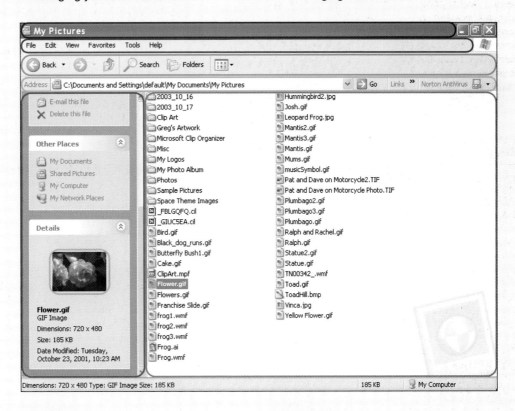

Preview

Unique to the My Pictures folder, you can preview a selected image file here. If the file preview cannot display, then a description of the image appears here instead.

List Box

Displays a listing of the folders and files within the current folder. To change the way in which items are listed in this box, see the section "Change the Folder List View" later in this chapter.

PREVIEW AN IMAGE

You can preview any saved image file using the Details feature in the My Pictures folder. The Details feature, located on the left task pane, also displays details about the file, such as the file type, dimensions, and modification date.

Autumn Leaves -
Dimensions: 720 x 480
Size: 185 KB
Date Modified: 10-23-03, 10:23

You can also use the Details feature to view images stored in *subfolders* — folders stored within the main My Pictures folder.

PREVIEW AN IMAGE

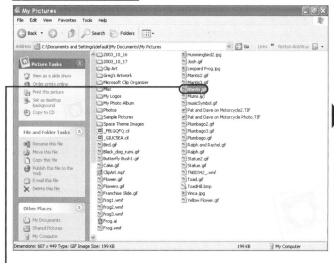

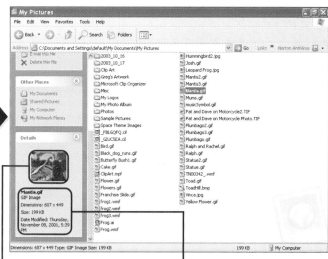

1 Click the image file you want to preview.

■ The Details area of the folder window shows a preview of the image.

Note: Depending on your screen resolution setting, you may need to scroll down to view the Details area.

■ Details about the image file appear here.

Note: To learn how to open the image into a larger viewing window, see Chapter 5.

CHANGE THE LIST VIEW

The list box area within the My Pictures window can display your image files in a variety of ways. For example, you can view your images as a list of filenames, as *thumbnails* — miniature versions of the full images — as icons, as tiles, and detailed lists. You can change your list view by clicking the Views button.

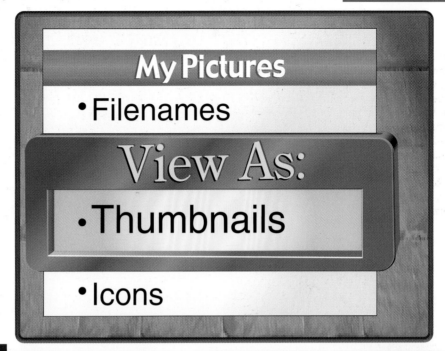

CHANGE THE LIST VIEW

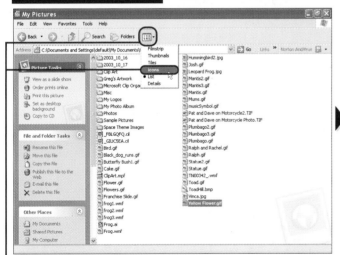

1 Click the **Views** button (▦).

2 Click a view.

Note: See the next section to learn more about using the Filmstrip view.

■ The list box area displays the files in the view format you selected.

■ In this example, the Icons view displays files and folders using icons.

VIEW IMAGES AS A FILMSTRIP

Windows XP enables you to view a group of images as a series of frames in a filmstrip. Unlike the other list views, the Filmstrip view allows you to see a larger preview of an image alongside a group of images.

VIEW IMAGES AS A FILMSTRIP

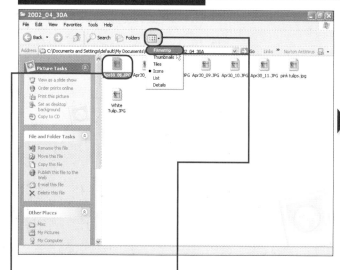

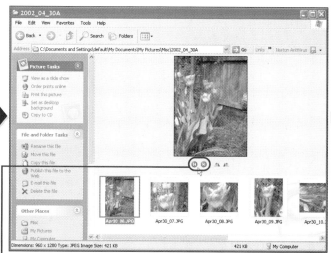

Note: If you store your snapshots in a special folder within the My Pictures window, open the folder containing the pictures.

1 Click an image in the group of images you want to view in Filmstrip view.

2 Click the **Views** button (▦▾).

3 Click **Filmstrip**.

■ The file list displays the files in Filmstrip view.

4 Click here to view another image.

■ Click the **Next Image** button (⬛) to advance to the next image.

■ Click the **Previous Image** button (⬛) to move back to the previous image.

■ You can also click the image you want to view.

How did my photo end up sideways?

When you take vertical shots with your digital camera, your photo appears sideways when you download the image to your computer. You may also have scanned the image vertically instead of horizontally. The rotate buttons can help you reposition the image for better viewing.

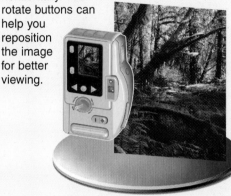

Can I also use the rotation commands on the shortcut menu?

Yes. If you right-click an image, the shortcut menu appears and lists the **Rotate Clockwise** and **Rotate Counter Clockwise** commands. You can select either command to rotate the image. You can only view these commands in the shortcut menu while viewing your images in Filmstrip view mode.

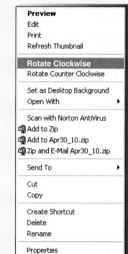

Preview
Edit
Print
Refresh Thumbnail

Rotate Clockwise
Rotate Counter Clockwise

Set as Desktop Background
Open With

Scan with Norton AntiVirus
Add to Zip
Add to Apr30_10.zip
Zip and E-Mail Apr30_10.zip

Send To

Cut
Copy

Create Shortcut
Delete
Rename

Properties

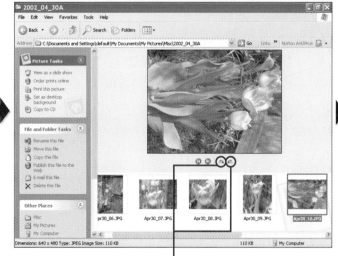

■ If your image displays sideways, you can click a rotation button to rotate the image in 90-degree increments.

■ Click the **Rotate Clockwise** button (🔄) to rotate the image in a clockwise direction.

■ Click the **Rotate Counterclockwise** button (🔄) to rotate the image in a counterclockwise direction.

■ The image rotates in the List view area.

Note: See the previous section to learn how to switch to other List views.

VIEW IMAGES AS A SLIDE SHOW

You can view the images
you store in the My
Pictures folder as a slide
show. The task pane
includes a link to activate
the slide show feature.
After you start the show,
the feature automatically
advances and displays
each image in the current
folder as a slide.

If the folder you want to view
holds a lot of photos, the slide
show may progress much
more slowly than a folder
containing just a few files.

VIEW IMAGES AS A SLIDE SHOW

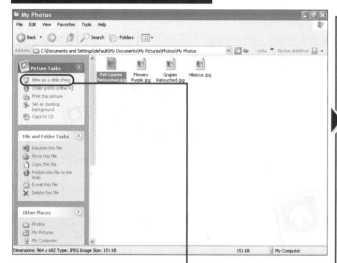

*Note: If you store your images
in a special folder within the My
Pictures window, open the folder
containing the pictures.*

1 Click **View as a slide
show**.

■ The first photo appears
as a slide, and each slide
advances automatically.

■ You can use the
navigation bar in the top-
right corner to control the
slide show manually.

■ You can also advance
each slide by clicking the
screen.

2 Click ⊗ to exit the slide
show.

■ You can also press `Esc` to
exit the slide show.

LAUNCH AN IMAGE-EDITING PROGRAM

When you want to edit an image stored in the My Pictures folder, you can specify a particular image-editing program with which you want to open the file.

Depending on the type of image-editing programs installed on your computer, your options may vary.

LAUNCH AN IMAGE-EDITING PROGRAM

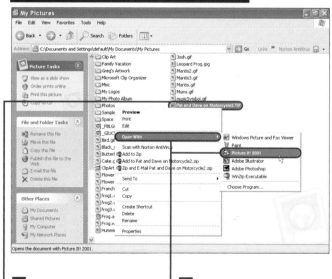

1 Right-click an image file.

2 Click **Open With**.

3 Click a program.

■ In this example, the Microsoft Picture It! program opens and displays the selected image file.

DELETE AN IMAGE

You can remove an image you no longer want by using the Delete task in the My Pictures folder. Once you activate the task, Windows XP displays a dialog box asking whether you really want to remove the file.

DELETE AN IMAGE

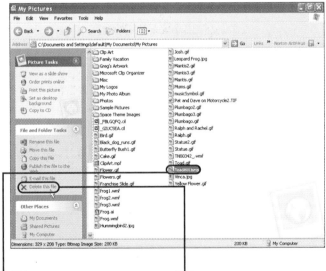

1 Click the image you want to remove.

2 Click **Delete this file**.

■ You can also press Delete on your keyboard.

■ A Confirm File Delete dialog box appears.

3 Click **Yes** to continue with the deletion.

■ You can click **No** to cancel the deletion.

■ The file moves from the folder to the Recycle Bin.

VIEW IMAGE PROPERTIES

You can view additional details about an image file using the file's Properties dialog box. The Properties dialog box lists information such as the creation date for the file, when it was last modified, and the download size and current size.

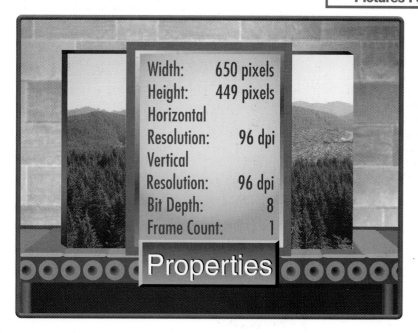

Width: 650 pixels
Height: 449 pixels
Horizontal Resolution: 96 dpi
Vertical Resolution: 96 dpi
Bit Depth: 8
Frame Count: 1

Properties

VIEW IMAGE PROPERTIES

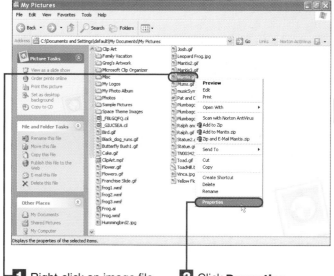

1 Right-click an image file.

2 Click **Properties**.

■ The file's Properties dialog box appears.

■ Information about the file displays here.

■ You can click the **Summary** tab to view details about image width, height, and bit depth.

■ You can toggle between viewing advanced properties and summary information by clicking the **Simple** or **Advanced** button.

3 Click **OK**.

■ The Properties dialog box closes.

PRINT AN IMAGE FILE

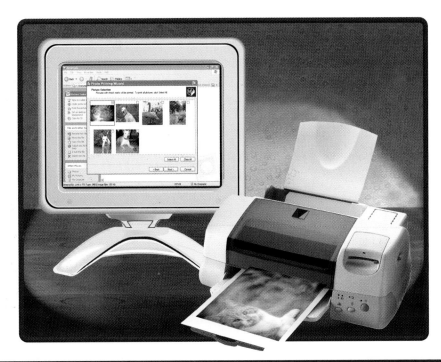

You can print an image from the My Pictures folder, or from any subfolder in the My Pictures folder. When you activate the Print this Picture task, the Photo Printing Wizard appears. You can follow the steps in the wizard dialog boxes to choose a printer and a layout, and to send the image to the printer.

PRINT AN IMAGE FILE

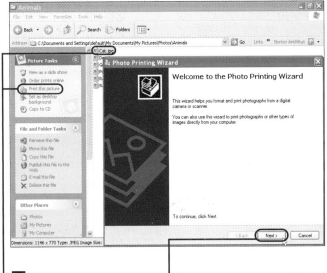

■ Click the image you want to print.

■ Click **Print this picture**.

■ The Photo Printing Wizard appears.

■ Click **Next**.

■ The Wizard places a check mark next to the image you selected for printing.

■ To print additional photos in the current folder, you can click other images you want to include in the printing process (☐ changes to ☑).

■ Click **Next**.

What type of paper should I use for my photo printouts?

Depending on the type of printer you are using, you can find a variety of photo-quality paper types for printing your digital photographs. Photo-quality paper is more expensive than multipurpose paper, but it is designed to create a more permanent image and improve the resolution and color of the printed images. Photo-quality paper comes in glossy and matte finishes, as well as variations of each. Be sure to select a photo-quality paper that your printer manufacturer recommends.

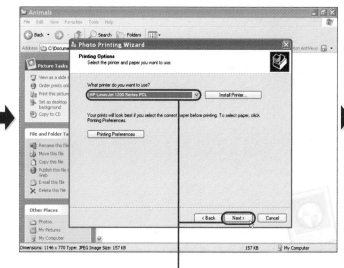

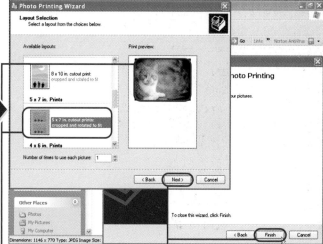

■ The Printing Options window appears.

■ If you use more than one printer with your computer, you can click ⌄ and select which printer you want to use.

5 Click **Next**.

■ The Layout Selection window appears.

6 Click the layout you want to use for the printed image.

■ The Wizard displays a preview of the printout.

7 Click **Next**.

■ The Wizard sends your image to the printer.

8 Click **Finish**.

■ The Photo Printing Wizard closes.

ORDER PRINTS ONLINE

You can turn your digital photographs into prints by placing an order on the Internet. You can open the Online Print Ordering Wizard, which guides you through each step you need to order a set of prints.

To use the Print Ordering Wizard, you must log on to your Internet connection. The Wizard offers you a list of several photo-developing companies from which you can choose. You can select from several printing options, then pay for the prints using a credit card.

ORDER PRINTS ONLINE

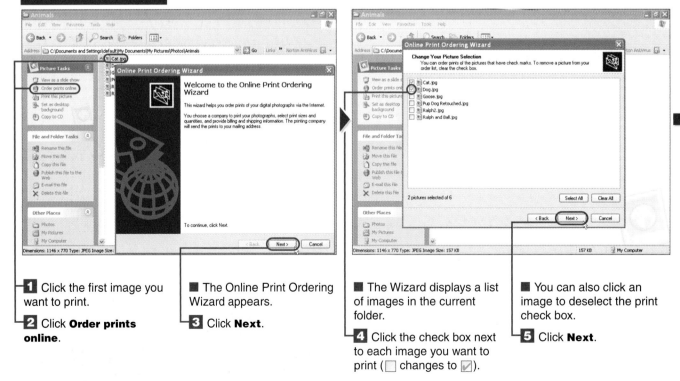

1 Click the first image you want to print.

2 Click **Order prints online**.

■ The Online Print Ordering Wizard appears.

3 Click **Next**.

■ The Wizard displays a list of images in the current folder.

4 Click the check box next to each image you want to print (☐ changes to ☑).

■ You can also click an image to deselect the print check box.

5 Click **Next**.

Are there other sources for online reprints?

Yes. You can choose from a variety of online photo services, such as Snapfish, Ofoto, and Bonusprint. You can conduct a simple Web search and find numerous online photo services. Most of these Web sites offer details on how to use the service, the cost, and when to expect delivery.

Can I take my memory stick to a photo-processing lab instead?

Yes. If you would rather not wait for your prints to arrive by mail, you can take your digital camera's memory card or stick to a photo-processing lab and have prints made while you wait. Many places feature a self-help kiosk you can use to select which images you want to print, along with options such as cropping and sizing.

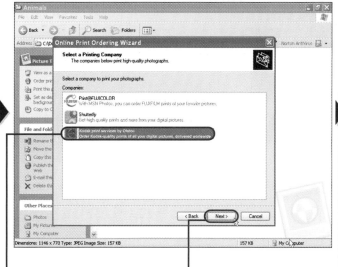

■ The Wizard displays a list of photo-developing companies.

6 Click the photo-developing company you want to use.

7 Click **Next**.

■ You may need to stop and connect to the Internet before proceeding.

■ The Wizard sends your selected prints to the online shopping cart and displays a list of prices for your order.

■ You can make changes to the quantities and print sizes.

■ Click here to remove a print from the selection.

8 Click **Next**.

■ Continue filling out the order form, including your payment method, to complete the process.

CHAPTER 4

Putting Images to Work in Windows XP

Not only can you organize your digital images in Windows XP, but you can also put them to work for you. This chapter shows you how to turn your photos into desktop wallpaper and screen savers as well as how to share your photos via e-mail and the Web.

TURN A PHOTO INTO DESKTOP WALLPAPER

You can use your digital images as *wallpaper* — the background that appears behind the shortcut icons and taskbar on your Windows XP desktop. For example, you can turn a family vacation photo or family pet snapshot into wallpaper. Turning photos into wallpaper allows you to customize and personalize Windows XP.

TURN A PHOTO INTO DESKTOP WALLPAPER

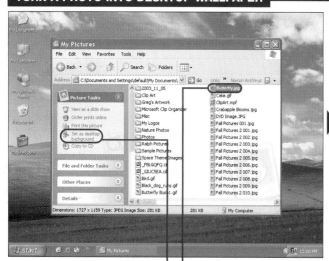

Note: To learn how to open the window, see Chapter 3.

SELECT DESKTOP WALLPAPER

1 Open the **My Pictures** folder window.

Note: To learn how to open the window, see Chapter 3.

■ If necessary, open the subfolder containing the image file you want to use as wallpaper.

2 Click the image file you want to use.

■ If you do not remember the image's filename, you can find the file by clicking 🔲▾ and then selecting **Thumbnails**.

3 Click **Set as desktop background**.

■ The photo appears as wallpaper on the computer desktop.

■ You can minimize the My Pictures window to see the entire desktop.

How do I remove wallpaper I no longer want?

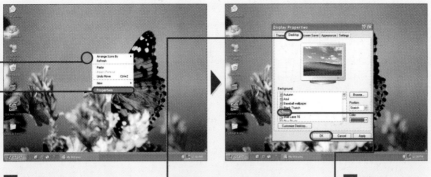

■ The new background appears on your desktop.

■ The previous background image no longer appears as a background option in the Display Properties dialog box.

1 Right-click over an empty area of the desktop.

2 Click **Properties**.

■ The Display Properties dialog box appears.

3 Click the **Desktop** tab.

4 Click another background.

5 Click **OK**.

ADJUST WALLPAPER PROPERTIES

1 Right-click the desktop.

2 Click **Properties**.

■ The Display Properties dialog box appears.

3 Click the **Desktop** tab.

4 Click the **Position** and select a position setting.

5 Click **OK**.

■ Windows XP applies the new position setting.

TURN PHOTOS INTO A SCREEN SAVER

You can display your digital photos as a screen saver in Windows XP. For example, you can take your favorite image files and turn them into a revolving slide show screen saver. Every time Windows XP activates the screen saver feature, your digital images appear one at a time.

TURN PHOTOS INTO A SCREEN SAVER

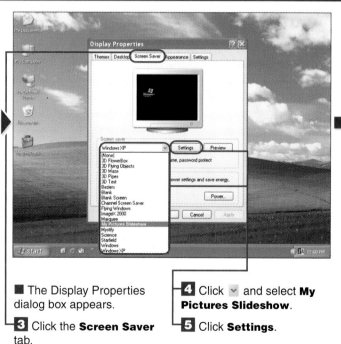

1 Right-click the desktop.

2 Click **Properties**.

■ The Display Properties dialog box appears.

3 Click the **Screen Saver** tab.

4 Click ∨ and select **My Pictures Slideshow**.

5 Click **Settings**.

Do I need to use a screen saver these days?

Screen savers once played an important part in keeping computer monitors safe from *screen burn* — a condition that occurred when a fixed image appeared on the screen for too long. Today's monitors are less susceptible to screen burn, but you can still apply a screen saver to keep your monitor safe, restrict access to your computer, and customize the appearance of your computer.

Can I preview the photo screen saver before applying it?

Yes. As soon as you select a screen saver from the list, the Display Properties dialog box shows you a miniature preview of the effect. For a larger preview, click the **Preview** button. To return to the dialog box after previewing the image, press any key or move the mouse.

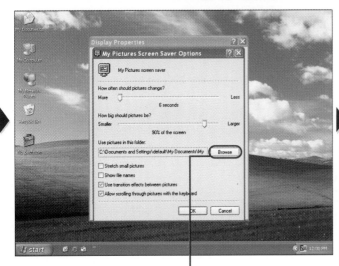

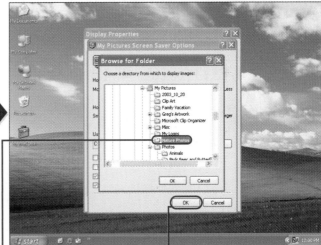

■ The My Pictures Screen Saver Options dialog box appears.

6 Click **Browse**.

■ The Browse for Folder dialog box appears.

7 Click the folder containing the photos you want to use.

Note: The folder must contain two or more image files.

■ If a listed folder contains subfolders, then double-click the folder name to view the contents of the subfolders.

8 Click **OK**.

CONTINUED➤

61

You can control different aspects of your screen saver feature. For example, you can specify how often the photos change as well as how large they appear.

TURN PHOTOS INTO A SCREEN SAVER (CONTINUED)

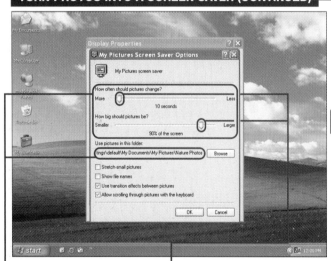

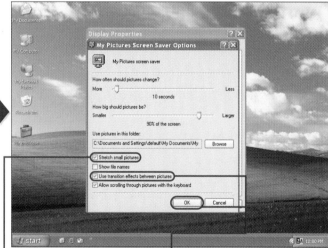

■ Windows XP returns you to the My Pictures Screen Saver Options dialog box.

■ The folder you selected in step **7** appears here.

9 Change any additional settings to adjust the appearance of the pictures.

■ Click and drag ☐ to change the duration of the picture display.

■ Click and drag ☐ to change the size of the pictures.

■ To make smaller photos appear larger, select this option (☐ changes to ☑).

■ By default, Windows XP adds a variety of transition effects to change from one photo to another in the screen saver. To turn off the effects, deselect this option (☑ changes to ☐).

10 Click **OK**.

How do I turn off the photo screen saver?

Open the Display Properties dialog box, click the Screen Saver tab, and then select another screen saver you want to apply from the list. Click **OK** to apply the new screen saver.

What are transition effects?

Transition effects control how one image changes into another. Transition effects are common in slide show programs, such as presentations you create using Microsoft PowerPoint. Windows XP applies a variety of transition effects to your screen saver slides. If you prefer to show one slide after another without any effects, you can turn the transition effects off in the My Pictures Screen Saver Options dialog box.

■ The Display Properties dialog box reappears.

■ A preview appears of the screen saver effect.

11 Click **OK**.

■ In this example, when the screen saver is activated, the photos appear one at a time.

MAKE A PHOTO ALBUM

You can place a group of photograph files in a single folder and tell Windows XP to treat them as a photo album. Windows XP applies the Photo Album template to the folder, which adds the Picture Tasks list to the task pane. With this template applied, you can also view the images using the Filmstrip view mode.

The Filmstrip view mode is not available in folders other than those that you create within the My Pictures folder unless you assign the Photo Album template. See Chapter 3 to learn more about using the Filmstrip view mode.

MAKE A PHOTO ALBUM

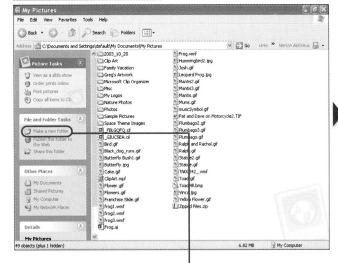

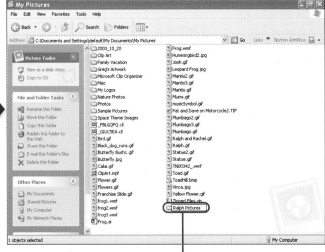

1 Open the **My Pictures** folder window.

2 Click **Make a new folder**.

■ A new folder appears in the current directory.

3 Type a name for the folder.

4 Press Enter.

What does a folder template do?

Each template type – documents, pictures, photos, and music – offers different ways in which you can view the folder contents, and different tasks that appear in the folder's pane area. To assign a folder template, follow these steps:

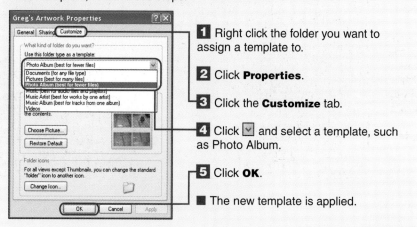

1 Right click the folder you want to assign a template to.

2 Click **Properties**.

3 Click the **Customize** tab.

4 Click ⬇ and select a template, such as Photo Album.

5 Click **OK**.

■ The new template is applied.

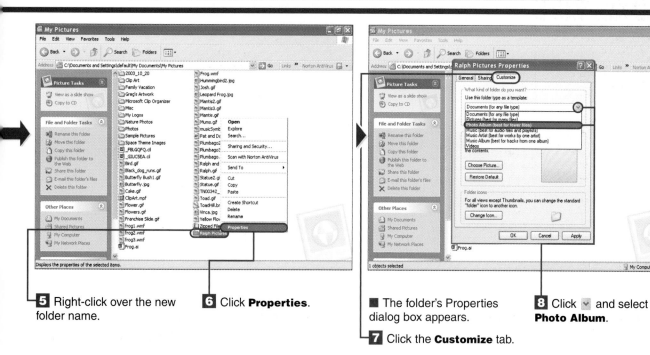

5 Right-click over the new folder name.

6 Click **Properties**.

■ The folder's Properties dialog box appears.

7 Click the **Customize** tab.

8 Click ⬇ and select **Photo Album**.

CONTINUED ▶

MAKE A PHOTO ALBUM

Turning a folder into a photo album gives you a convenient place to store and view related images. For example, you can place photos from a child's birthday party into a single photo album folder so that you can easily find them later and keep them separate from the other images that you store on your computer.

MAKE A PHOTO ALBUM (CONTINUED)

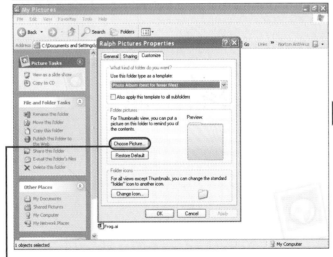

9 Click **Choose Picture**.

■ The Browse dialog box appears.

10 Select a photo you want to appear on the front of the folder.

■ You can click the Look in ⌄ and navigate to the folder containing the picture you want to use.

11 Click **Open**.

Do I need to assign a picture to my folder?

Only if you want to. For example, if the folder is a photo album of vacation pictures, then you can add one of the images to the front of the folder to help you identify the folder's contents. When you view the folder listing using the Thumbnails view, you can see the folder image. See Chapter 3 to learn more about view modes for viewing files and folders in the file list.

Can I use my photo album as a screen saver?

Yes. After you assign the photo album template and place your images in the folder, you can use the images in the folder as a screen saver. See the section "Turn Photos Into a Screen Saver" in this chapter. You can also turn any selected image in the folder into desktop wallpaper. See the section "Turn a Photo Into Desktop Wallpaper" to learn more.

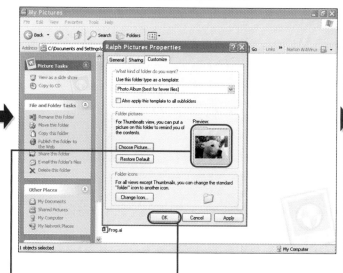

■ The image appears on the front of the folder.

■ Adding a photo to the folder cover can help you readily identify its contents later.

12 Click **OK**.

13 Click the **Views** button (▦▾).

14 Click **Thumbnails**.

■ The image you assigned appears on the front of the folder.

■ You can now move or copy photos to the new album.

SHARE PHOTOS ON YOUR COMPUTER

If you share your computer with other users, then you can also share photos by storing them in the Shared Documents folder. Unlike the personal My Documents folders, which are available only to the person logged on at the time, the Shared Documents folder is accessible to all users.

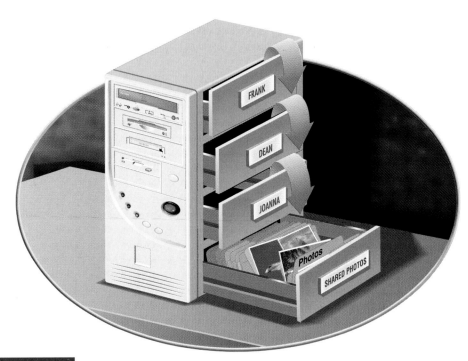

SHARE PHOTOS ON YOUR COMPUTER

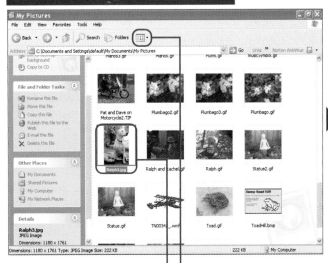 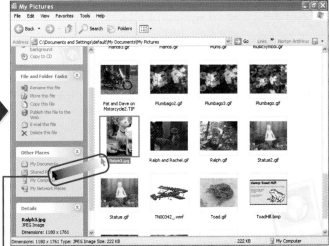

1 Open the folder that contains the photo you want to share.

■ You can click 🔳▾ to select Thumbnails, Icon, Details, or List view.

2 Click the photo to select it.

3 Drag the photo file and drop it on the **Shared Pictures** link.

Note: If the Shared Pictures link does not appear, then you can cut and paste the image into the Shared Pictures folder inside the Shared Documents folder instead.

How do I remove a photo from the Shared Pictures folder?

To remove a folder, follow these steps:

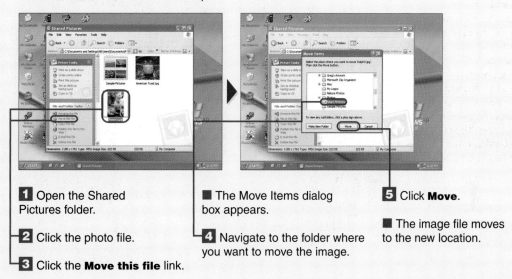

1 Open the Shared Pictures folder.

2 Click the photo file.

3 Click the **Move this file** link.

■ The Move Items dialog box appears.

4 Navigate to the folder where you want to move the image.

5 Click **Move**.

■ The image file moves to the new location.

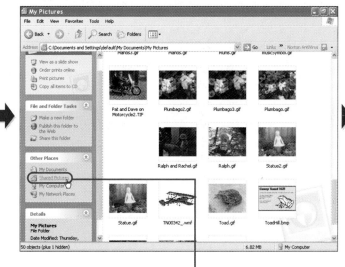

■ Windows XP adds the photo to the Shared Pictures folder.

4 Click the **Shared Pictures** link.

■ The file you designated as a shared photo now appears in the Shared Pictures folder list.

E-MAIL A PHOTO

You can e-mail any photo that you store in the My Pictures folder. In fact, the folder window includes a special task link for this action. The e-mail feature allows you to reduce the image size before sending the image, or to send it at the original size.

Photographs and other image files are much bigger in file size, so they can take a long time to send in ane-mail.

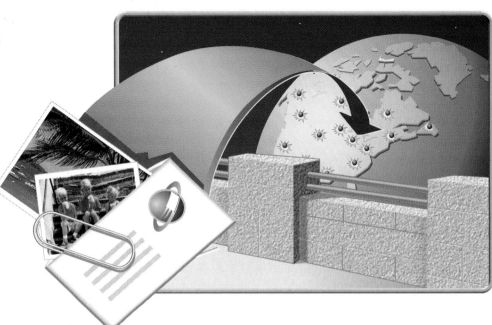

E-MAIL A PHOTO

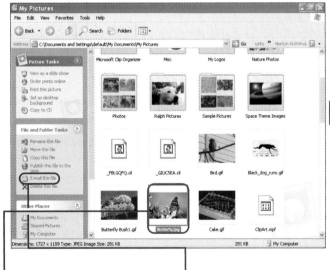

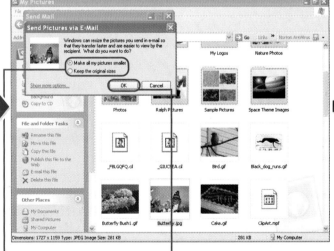

1 Click the photo you want to e-mail.

2 Click the **E-mail this file** link.

■ The Send Pictures via E-mail dialog box appears.

3 Click a size option (○ changes to ◉).

■ Click the **Make all my pictures smaller** option to reduce the image file size for e-mailing.

■ Click the **Keep the original sizes** option if you want to send the original image size.

4 Click **OK**.

Are there other ways to reduce the image file size?

Yes. You can use a file compression utility to compress, or zip, your image files. There are a variety of compression utilities you can download from the Internet, such as WinZip, EnZip, and ZipGenius.

Windows XP also includes a feature for creating a compressed folder, where any file you place within the folder is compressed. If you do not already use a file compression utility, then follow these steps to access the Windows XP tool:

1 In the My Pictures folder window, click **File**.

2 Click **New**.

3 Click **Compressed (zipped) Folder**.

■ Windows XP creates a compressed folder, identified by a zipper icon.

■ You can change the folder name, if you want.

■ To compress your image files, drag them to the new folder.

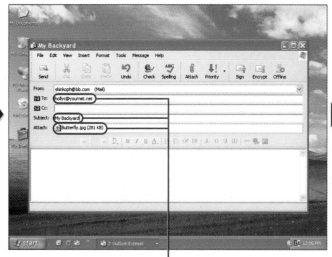

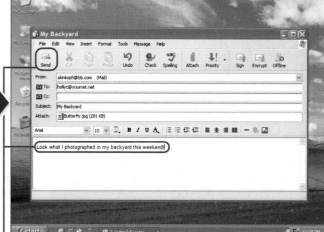

■ Outlook Express opens with a new window for your e-mail message.

Note: If you use another default e-mail program, it may open instead of Outlook Express.

■ The photo appears as a file attachment.

5 Type the e-mail address of the person to whom you want to send the photo.

6 Type a subject for the message.

7 Type the message text you want to accompany the photo.

8 Click **Send**.

■ Outlook Express sends your message and photo.

Note: If you are not currently connected to the Internet, a dialog box may appear, prompting you to log onto your Internet account.

PUBLISH A PICTURE TO THE MSN WEB SITE

You can publish your digital pictures to the Web so other people can view them. For example, you can use the Web Publishing Wizard to publish your photos to the MSN service provider. The Web Publishing Wizard guides you through the necessary steps for setting up an account and uploading your photos.

PUBLISH A PICTURE TO THE MSN WEB SITE

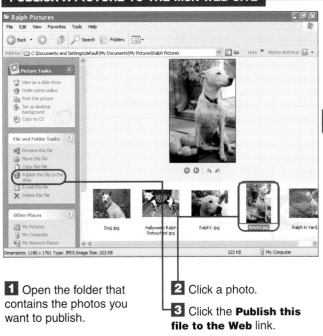

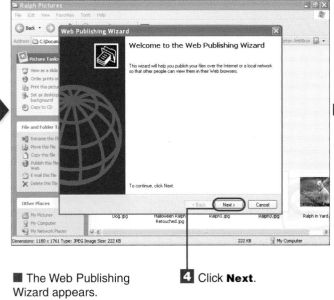

1 Open the folder that contains the photos you want to publish.

2 Click a photo.

3 Click the **Publish this file to the Web** link.

■ The Web Publishing Wizard appears.

4 Click **Next**.

How do I add copyright information to a photo?

Right-click the filename and click **Properties** to open the Properties dialog box. Click the **Summary** tab and click the **Simple** button to display the Summary text boxes. Fill out the text boxes with the information you want to include with the file and click **OK**.

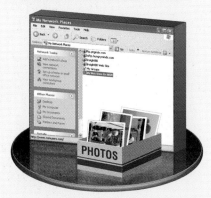

Can I publish an entire folder of photos?

Yes. The Wizard dialog box lists all the photos in the current folder. Just select the photos in the list that you want Windows XP to publish. Photos with check marks next to them indicate that they are selected for publishing.

■ A check mark appears next to your photo.

■ Click the check box next to any additional photos you want to publish (☐ changes to ☑).

5 Click **Next**.

6 Click a service account you want to host your photos.

7 Click **Next**.

CONTINUED

PUBLISH A PICTURE TO THE MSN WEB SITE

MSN Groups offers you a free and easy way to share your digital photos with others by posting them on the MSN Web site. In order to use this feature, you must first set up an account with MSN Groups. You can use a Wizard to set up your account so that you can have a place to store and view your online photos.

Individual photos cannot exceed 1MB, or megabyte, in size. MSN Groups supports GIF, JPEG, TIF, BMP, and PNG file formats.

PUBLISH A PICTURE TO THE MSN WEB SITE (CONTINUED)

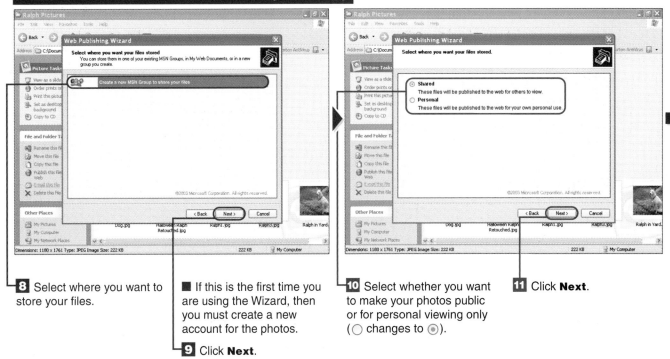

8 Select where you want to store your files.

■ If this is the first time you are using the Wizard, then you must create a new account for the photos.

9 Click **Next**.

10 Select whether you want to make your photos public or for personal viewing only (○ changes to ◉).

11 Click **Next**.

What is the difference between shared and personal viewing?

The difference is whether you allow others to view the photos or just yourself. For example, you can choose the Personal option and use the MSN Groups site to keep a digital photo safe in case your computer crashes. With the Personal option, only you can view the photos. Keep in mind that storage is limited; a single photo cannot exceed 1MB, and your total storage is limited to 3MB. If you want others to view your photos, you must select the Shared option. You can then share the assigned Web site address with others so they can view the photos.

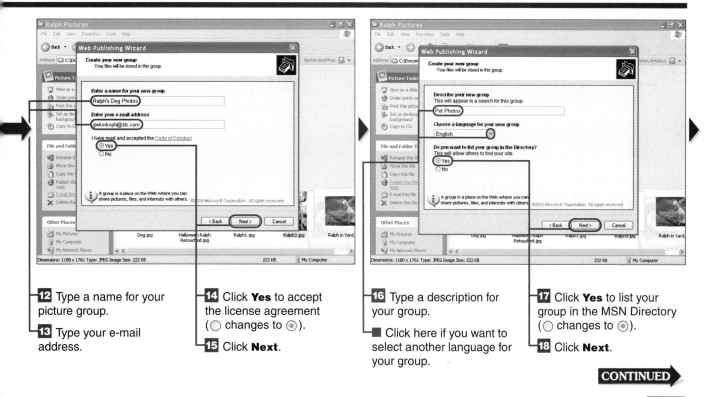

12 Type a name for your picture group.

13 Type your e-mail address.

14 Click **Yes** to accept the license agreement (⃝ changes to ⦿).

15 Click **Next**.

16 Type a description for your group.

■ Click here if you want to select another language for your group.

17 Click **Yes** to list your group in the MSN Directory (⃝ changes to ⦿).

18 Click **Next**.

CONTINUED

PUBLISH A PICTURE TO THE MSN WEB SITE

After you complete the steps for creating an MSN Groups account, the Wizard helps you upload your photo. When you have uploaded the photo, you can view the image file using your Web browser.

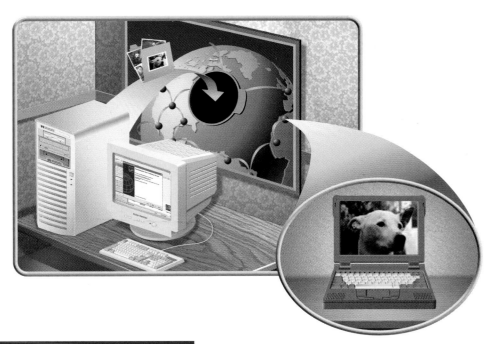

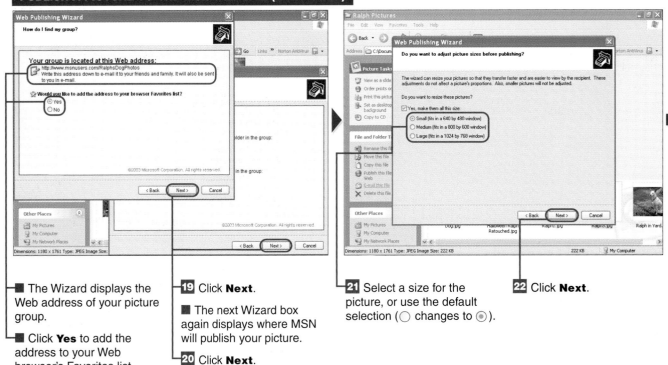

■ The Wizard displays the Web address of your picture group.

■ Click **Yes** to add the address to your Web browser's Favorites list (○ changes to ⊙).

19 Click **Next**.

■ The next Wizard box again displays where MSN will publish your picture.

20 Click **Next**.

21 Select a size for the picture, or use the default selection (○ changes to ⊙).

22 Click **Next**.

How do I add to my online pictures?

You can open the Wizard dialog box to publish more photos to your MSN group. Instead of guiding you through the procedure to set up a group for the first time, the Wizard lists your current group and helps you upload photos to the existing storage site. You can also add and remove photos in the browser window by clicking the links on your group page. You may need to install some additional software from the MSN site to add and remove photos from the Web.

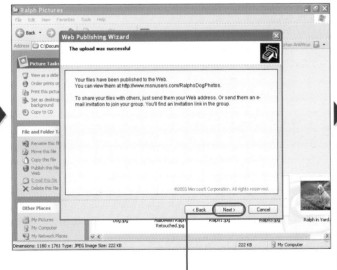

■ The Wizard uploads your file and displays additional information about your Web site.

23 Click **Next**.

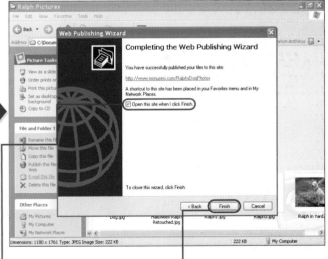

■ The final Wizard window appears.

■ Leave this option selected to immediately view your published file in a Web browser.

24 Click **Finish**.

■ Your Web browser appears, and displays the published picture.

FTP A PICTURE TO A WEB FOLDER

If you already have a Web page, then you can use Windows XP to transfer a picture to your Web folder. Using *File Transfer Protocol,* or FTP, you can upload documents and image files from your computer to the Web server that stores your Web pages.

You can use the Add Network Place Wizard to help you set up Windows XP to work with your FTP site. After creating an Internet connection in your My Network Places folder, you can use the connection to transfer files.

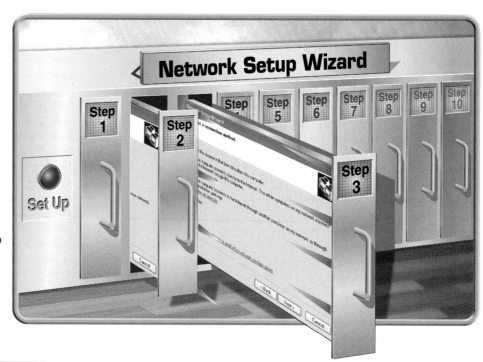

FTP A PICTURE TO A WEB FOLDER

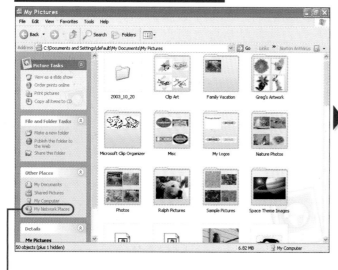

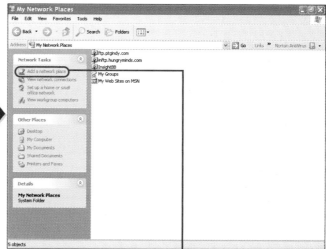

CREATE A NEW NETWORK PLACE

1 Click the **My Network Places** link.

■ The My Network Places folder window appears.

2 Click the **Add a network place** link.

Can I use a network connection I previously set up?

Yes. The My Network Places folder keeps track of your network connections and lists them in the folder window. To access a connection at any time, simply double-click the network name. Like the other folder windows, the My Network Places folder includes a task pane with links to common functions and folders.

Can I create a network place on MSN?

Yes. If you do not currently have an established Web site on a server, then you can set up space on the MSN site. The Add Network Place Wizard includes MSN Communities in the list of service providers to which you can connect. Your steps for creating an account may vary from those that appear in this section. To learn more about setting up an MSN Web site, see the previous section, "Publish a Picture to the MSN Web Site."

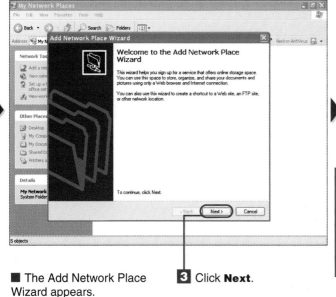

■ The Add Network Place Wizard appears.

3 Click **Next**.

4 Click the **Choose another network location** option.

5 Click **Next**.

CONTINUED ▶

FTP A PICTURE TO A WEB FOLDER

When you create a new Network Place, you must specify the Internet or network address for the site to which you want to connect. The Add Network Place Wizard guides you through the process of specifying your username and creating a unique name for the connection in the My Network Places folder.

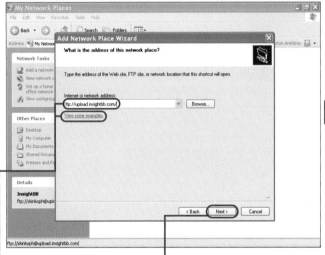

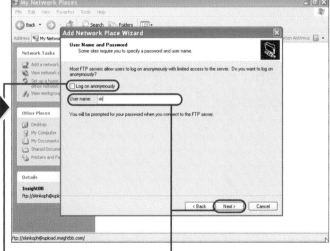

6 Type the address of your Internet service provider's server or network.

■ Click here if you need some examples of how to type in the address.

Note: If you do not know the network address, then you can contact your Internet service provider to learn more about the exact path for accessing network or Web folders.

7 Click **Next**.

8 Deselect the **Log on anonymously** check box option (☑ changes to ☐).

■ If you log onto your account's server anonymously, then you can leave this option selected. Most servers require a logon name and password to access their server files.

9 Type your username.

10 Click **Next**.

How do I stop the Wizard from adding a network place?

To end the Add Network Place Wizard at any time, just click **Cancel**. This stops the process completely, and no new network place is created. If you want to add the network place again, then you must reopen the Wizard and start from the beginning. If you only need to return to a previous dialog box, rather than exit entirely, then you can click **Back**.

How do I find out my username and password for my FTP server?

Generally, you create a username and password when you sign up for a Web storage account with your Internet service provider. If you lost your information, then you must contact your provider to retrieve the username and password. A few FTP servers allow you to log on anonymously, in which case you can leave the Log on anonymously check box selected in step **8**.

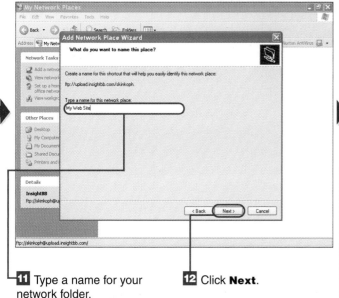

11 Type a name for your network folder.

12 Click **Next**.

■ The last wizard dialog box appears.

13 Deselect the **Open this network place when I click Finish** check box option (☑ changes to ☐).

■ You can leave this option selected if you want to immediately access the site.

14 Click **Finish**.

■ The Wizard establishes a new network connection in the My Network Places folder window.

FTP A PICTURE TO A WEB FOLDER

Once you have created a
network connection, you
can return to the My
Network Places folder
any time and use the
Windows XP FTP
feature. One of the
easiest ways to upload
files is through the Copy
and Paste commands.
Windows XP treats
the FTP folder just
like a folder on your
computer's hard drive.

FTP A PICTURE TO A WEB FOLDER (CONTINUED)

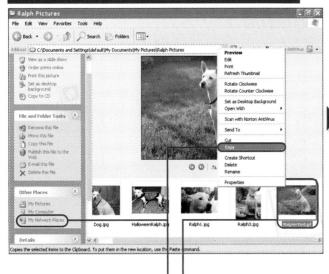

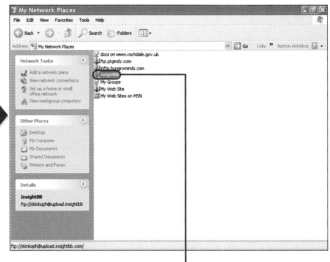

FTP A PICTURE

1 Open the folder that
contains a photo you want
to upload.

2 Right-click over the
image or icon.

3 Click **Copy**.

4 Click the **My Network
Places** link.

■ The My Network Places
folder window appears.

5 Double-click the network
connection you want to
open.

What other programs can I use to FTP my photos to a server?

If you are looking for more powerful FTP tools, then consider using an FTP utility. There are numerous FTP utilities available today, including CuteFTP (www.globalscape. com), WS_FTP (www. ipswitch.com,) and AceFTP freeware (freeware.aceftp.com). FTP utilities offer more options and commands for uploading and managing files on any server. To find FTP utilities, you can conduct a Web search for *FTP utilities* or *FTP software* using your favorite search engine. Many software companies offer trial versions you can use before you buy them. You can download free versions of FTP utilities as well.

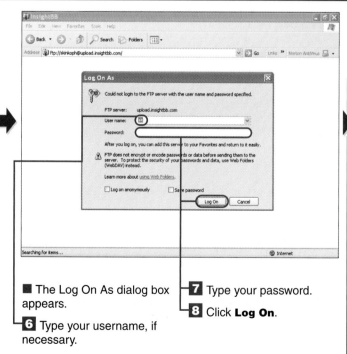

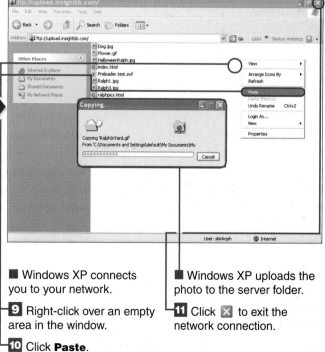

■ The Log On As dialog box appears.

6 Type your username, if necessary.

7 Type your password.

8 Click **Log On**.

■ Windows XP connects you to your network.

9 Right-click over an empty area in the window.

10 Click **Paste**.

■ Windows XP uploads the photo to the server folder.

11 Click ☒ to exit the network connection.

CHAPTER 5

Viewing Photos with the Windows Picture and Fax Viewer

You can quickly see the photos that you have stored on your computer using Windows Picture and Fax Viewer, a program that installs with Windows XP. This chapter shows you how you can view and work with photos using the viewer window.

DISPLAY A PHOTO

You can use the Windows Picture and Fax Viewer program to view photographs and other images you store on your computer. This program saves you the time of having to open a separate image-editing program just to view a single image. Once you open the viewer window, you can navigate between photos in the same folder.

You can activate the Windows Picture and Fax Viewer program from within the My Documents or My Computer windows and access photos from any folder on your computer's hard drive.

DISPLAY A PHOTO

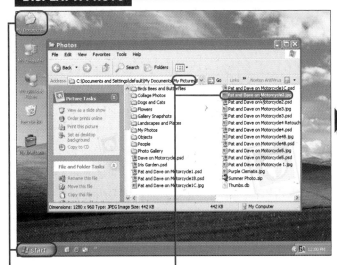

1 Double-click the **My Documents** icon.

■ You can also click the **start** button on the taskbar and then click **My Documents** to open the My Documents window.

2 Open the folder containing the photo you want to view.

Note: See Chapter 3 to learn more about viewing images with the My Pictures folder.

3 Double-click the photo.

■ Windows XP displays the photo in the Windows Picture and Fax Viewer window.

4 Click the **Next Image** button (■).

Note: If the current folder does not contain additional image files, clicking the Next Image button does not display additional photos.

Which file types can I open in the Windows Picture and Fax Viewer window?

You can open numerous kinds of image files, including bitmap files and vector files. For example, you can open GIF, JPEG, TIFF, PCX, BMP, and PNG files in the viewer, all of which are bitmap files. You can also open WMF, EMF, and PICT vector files.

Where should I store all my photographs and image files?

To make files easy to find, Windows XP automatically creates a My Pictures subfolder within the My Documents folder. You can use the My Pictures folder to store your photos in one place. You can easily create additional folders within the My Pictures folder to keep your image files organized. See Chapter 3 to learn more about using the My Pictures folder.

■ The Viewer displays the next consecutive image file in the folder.

5 Click the **Previous Image** button ( ).

■ The Viewer displays the previous image file.

6 When you have finished viewing the photo, click ☒.

■ The Viewer window closes.

CHANGE THE IMAGE MAGNIFICATION

You can use the Windows Picture and Fax Viewer's toolbar buttons to zoom in to enlarge or zoom out to reduce your view of any photo currently showing in the window. You can zoom in for a closer look, or zoom out to see more of the photo. You can also choose to view the image in the current window size or without scaling.

CHANGE THE IMAGE MAGNIFICATION

1 Click the **Zoom In** button (🔍).

■ The viewer zooms in to magnify the photo.

■ You can click the button multiple times to continue zooming in.

How do I resize the Windows Picture and Fax Viewer window?

For fast resizing, you can click the **Maximize** button ( ), located in the top right corner of the window. You can also move the mouse pointer over the border of the window, and then click and drag the border to resize the viewer.

Is there a keyboard shortcut for zooming in or out?

Yes. You can press the Plus Sign key ( ) on the numeric keypad on your keyboard to quickly zoom in to see the image magnified. You can press the Minus Sign key ( ) on the numeric keypad to zoom out again.

2 Click the **Zoom Out** button ( ).

■ The viewer zooms out to reduce the magnification.

■ You can click the button multiple times to continue zooming out.

■ Depending on the type of image, you can click the **Best Fit** button ( ) to zoom in or zoom out of the image to fit the viewer's window size.

■ You can also click the **Actual Size** button ( ) to display the image at 100 percent magnification.

■ This example applies the Actual Size tool.

VIEW A SLIDE SHOW

If you place more than
one photograph file in
the same folder, you can
quickly view the images
as a slide show using the
Windows Picture and Fax
Viewer. When viewing
images as a slide show,
each image appears as a
slide or full-screen image
on the monitor screen.

VIEW A SLIDE SHOW

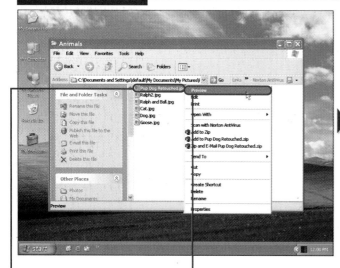

1 Right-click the first photo
you want to view as a slide
show image.

2 Click **Preview**.

■ Windows Picture and Fax
Viewer opens.

*Note: See the section "Display a
Photo" to learn more about using the
Windows Picture and Fax Viewer
window.*

3 Click the **Start Slide
Show** button (🖼).

Can I pre-select which photos to use in the slide show?

Yes. You can select multiple files and then right-click one filename to open the Windows Picture and Fax Viewer as outlined in the steps below. Then you can activate the slide show and display only the slides you selected. To select multiple files, press and hold the [Ctrl] key while clicking each image file you want to include in the slide show.

Can I make changes to an image before I start a slide show?

You can make some rudimentary changes to an image using the default image-editing program, Windows Paint. When you click the **Edit Image** button () in the Windows Picture and Fax Viewer window, the Windows Paint program opens automatically and displays the current image for editing.

■ Each photo in the folder appears briefly as a slide in the slide show.

■ You can manually advance each image by clicking the screen.

■ You can also use the navigation bar to advance the slides.

■ Click the **Next Picture** button ([◎]) to advance to the next slide.

■ Click the **Previous Picture** button ([◎]) to return to the previous slide.

■ Click the **Pause Slide Show** button ([◎]) to pause the slide show.

■ Click the **Start Slide Show** button ([◎]) to restart the slide show after pausing.

4 Click the **Close the Window** button ([◎]) to exit the slide show.

■ You can also press [Esc] to exit the slide show.

ROTATE A PHOTO

If you scan an original image in the wrong orientation, you can quickly remedy the problem by rotating the image in the Windows Picture and Fax Viewer window. You can rotate images in 90-degree increments in a clockwise or counterclockwise direction.

ROTATE A PHOTO

1 Click a rotation button.

■ Click the **Rotate Clockwise** button (🔼) to rotate the image to the left.

■ Click the **Rotate Counterclockwise** button (🔼) to rotate the image to the right.

■ The Viewer rotates the image.

■ You can click the rotation buttons multiple times to continue rotating the image.

DELETE A PHOTO

You can remove a photo
you no longer want to
store on your computer.
When you delete a photo,
the Windows Picture and
Fax Viewer removes the
image from the current
folder and sends it to your
Windows XP Recycle Bin.

DELETE A PHOTO

1 Display the photo you
want to delete.

2 Click the **Delete**
button (⊠).

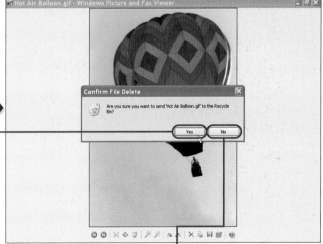

■ A Confirm File Delete
dialog box appears.

3 Click **Yes** to continue
with the deletion.

■ You can click **No** to cancel
the deletion.

COPY A PHOTO

You can create a copy of a photograph file from within the Windows Picture and Fax Viewer window. You may want to copy a photo image to make edits to the image without changing the original photo file.

When copying a photo, you can save the image in the BMP, JPEG, GIF, TIFF, or PNG format.

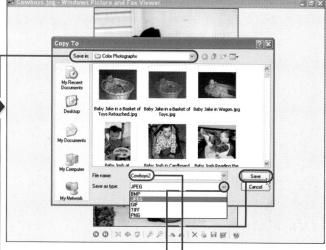

1 Display the photo you want to copy.

2 Click the **Copy To** button (📷).

■ The Copy To dialog box appears.

3 Specify a folder in which you want to store the copy, or save the image in the default folder.

■ You can click the **Save In** ☑ and select another folder.

4 Type a new name for the image.

■ You can click the **Save as type** ☑ and select another file type.

5 Click **Save**.

■ The Viewer saves the file.

VIEW IMAGE PROPERTIES

You can view the
properties of an image
in the Windows Picture
and Fax Viewer to learn
more about the image.
File properties include
information about when
the file was created, the
size of the file, and the
file's location.

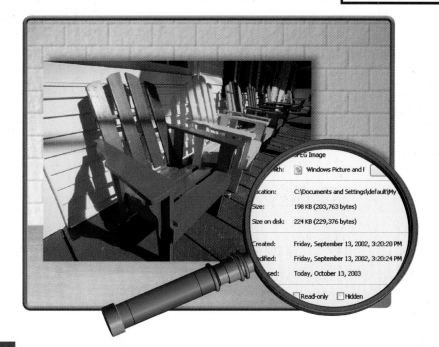

VIEW IMAGE PROPERTIES

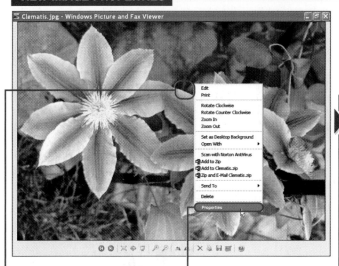

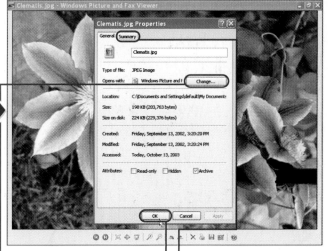

1 Right-click the image.

2 Click **Properties**.

■ The file's Properties
dialog box appears.

■ Information about the file
appears here.

■ If you prefer to view the
image with another image-
editing program instead of
the Windows Picture and
Fax Viewer, you can click
here and select a program.

■ You can click the
Summary tab to view details
about image width, height,
and other image properties.

3 Click **OK**.

■ The Properties dialog box
closes.

ANNOTATE A TIFF FILE

If you view a TIFF file in the Windows Picture and Fax Viewer window, additional tools enable you to add notes about the image or point out areas that you want to fix.

Annotation tools come in handy when viewing fax files in Windows XP. For example, you can add notes to a fax in the viewer window and hand the printed document to a coworker for additional input.

ANNOTATE A TIFF FILE

Note: See the section "Copy a Photo" to learn how to save an image as a TIFF file type.

■ When displaying a TIFF image, the Viewer displays additional annotation tools for adding information to the image.

ADD A HIGHLIGHT

1 Click the **New Highlight Annotation** button ( ).

2 Click and drag a marquee where you want to highlight the image.

■ A yellow highlight box appears on the image.

■ You can select from these tools to draw an outline box, a regular box, a freeform line, or a straight line on the image.

Can I select a font color for my annotation text?

Yes. Click the **Edit Info** button () to open the Font dialog box. You can select a font, font style, and size, as well as change the color of the annotation text. When you finish making your selections, click **OK** to view your changes.

How do I remove an annotation I no longer want?

Click the **Select Annotation** button (⬚) and then click the annotation item you want to remove. Click the **Delete** button (⊠) or press **Delete** on the keyboard to remove the item from the image.

ADD TEXT

3 Click the **New Text Annotation** button (Ⓐ).

4 Click and drag a marquee where you want to add a text box to the image.

5 Double-click the text box.

6 Type the text you want to add.

■ Click outside the text box to view the text as it appears on the image.

■ To add a note text box instead of a regular text box, select this tool.

■ When you close the viewer window, you can save your annotations along with the image file.

PRINT A PHOTO

You can print any photo
you view in the Windows
Picture and Fax Viewer
window. You can use the
Photo Printing Wizard to
help you determine the
page layout of the printed
image. For example, you
may choose to print the
photo as a full-page image
or as a 5" x 7" print.

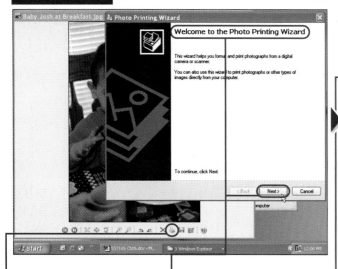

1 Display the photo you
want to print.

2 Click the **Print**
button (🖼).

■ The Photo Printing Wizard
appears.

3 Click **Next**.

4 If the check box next
to the photo you want to
print is empty, select it
(☐ changes to ☑).

■ To print additional photos
in the current folder, you can
click the check box next to
each photo that you want to
include in the printing
process.

5 Click **Next**.

How do I select the paper source I want to use for my printout?

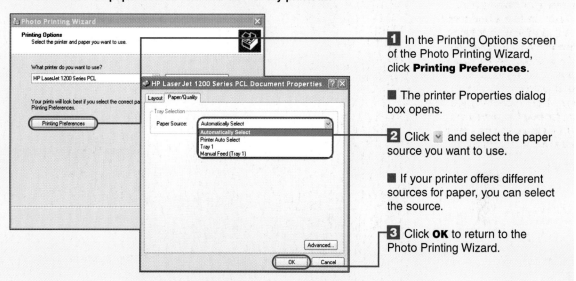

1 In the Printing Options screen of the Photo Printing Wizard, click **Printing Preferences**.

■ The printer Properties dialog box opens.

2 Click ⌄ and select the paper source you want to use.

■ If your printer offers different sources for paper, you can select the source.

3 Click **OK** to return to the Photo Printing Wizard.

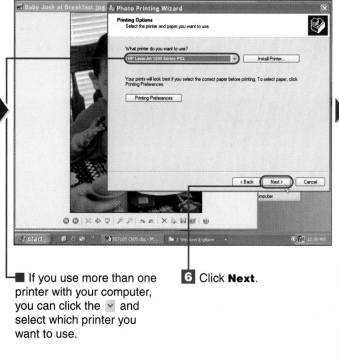

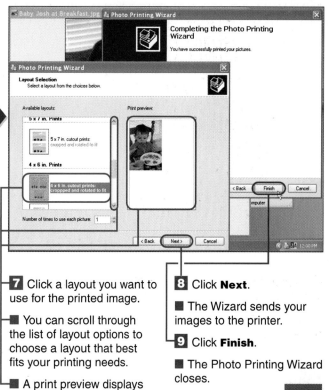

■ If you use more than one printer with your computer, you can click the ⌄ and select which printer you want to use.

6 Click **Next**.

7 Click a layout you want to use for the printed image.

■ You can scroll through the list of layout options to choose a layout that best fits your printing needs.

■ A print preview displays here.

8 Click **Next**.

■ The Wizard sends your images to the printer.

9 Click **Finish**.

■ The Photo Printing Wizard closes.

99

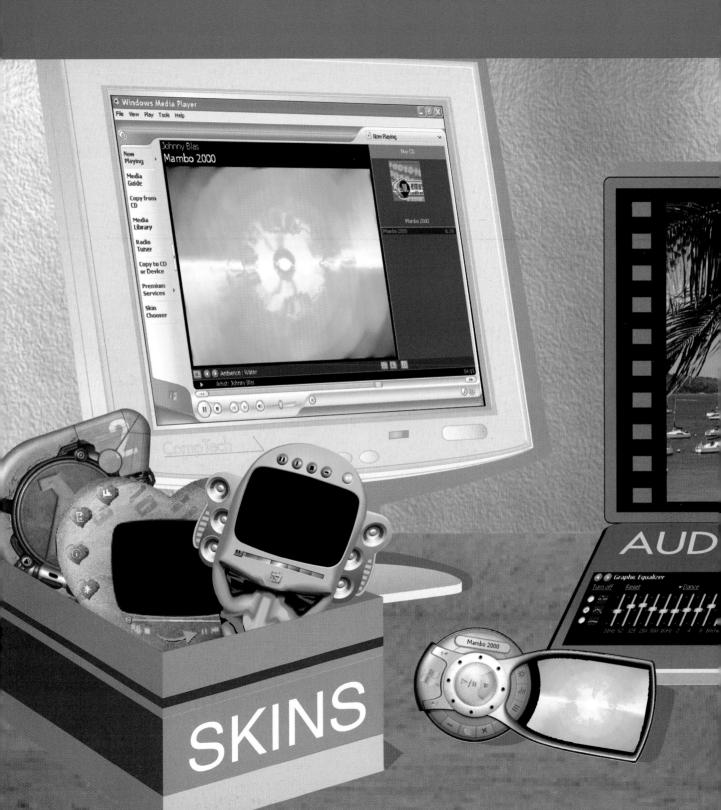

CHAPTER 6

Setting Up Windows Media Player

You can use Windows Media Player to listen to your favorite CDs, tune into Internet broadcasts, and view DVDs. This chapter shows you how to customize Windows Media Player to meet your specific requirements.

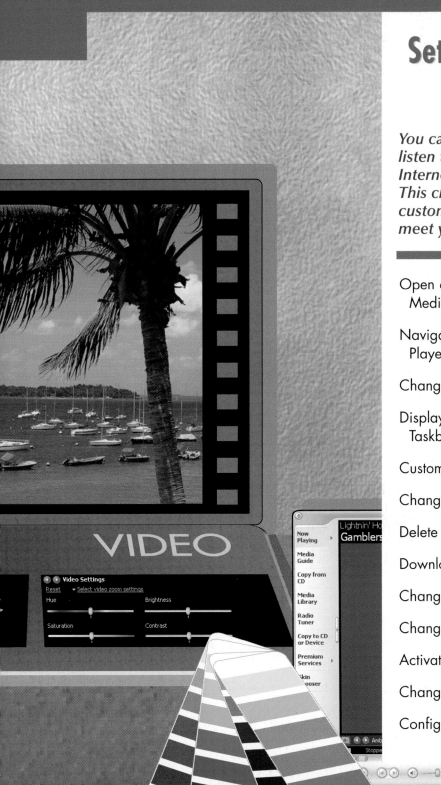

Windows XP includes Windows Media Player to allow you to play back and record audio as well as to view video. To begin using the program, you must first learn how to find and open the Windows Media Player window. When you finish using the program, you can close the Windows Media Player window to free up computer processing power.

OPEN AND CLOSE WINDOWS MEDIA PLAYER

OPEN WINDOWS MEDIA PLAYER

1 Click **start**.

2 Click **All Programs**.

3 Click **Windows Media Player**.

■ The Windows Media Player window appears, displaying the Media Guide page.

Note: You may need to connect to the Internet in order to view all the Media Guide page links.

■ By default, the Windows Media Player window appears at a reduced size in Full mode. You can resize or maximize the window.

4 Click **Show Menu Bar** (⊙).

Can I leave Windows Media Player open while I work with other programs?

Yes. You can minimize the Windows Media Player window to run in the background while you work with other programs or tasks. You can also use the new Mini Player toolbar to keep the program open, but minimized to a playback toolbar on your Windows XP desktop taskbar. See the section "Activate the Mini Player Toolbar" to use this feature.

How do I find the latest version of Windows Media Player?

To check which version of the program you have, click the **Help** menu and click **About Windows Media Player**. To upgrade to the latest version, click **Help**, and then click **Check for Player Updates**. You can then connect to the Internet and download the latest program version.

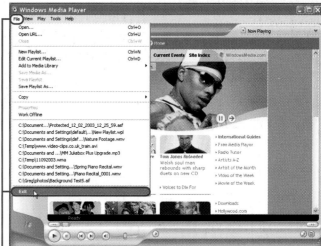

■ A regular menu bar appears, with a regular window border around the Windows Media Player window.

■ You can click **Hide Menu Bar** (⊙) to hide the window border again.

CLOSE WINDOWS MEDIA PLAYER

-1 Click **File**.

-2 Click **Exit**.

■ You can also click the window's ☒ button.

■ The Windows Media Player window closes.

NAVIGATE THE WINDOWS MEDIA PLAYER WINDOW

When you view Windows Media Player in Full mode, you can access all of the program's features. It is a good idea to familiarize yourself with the onscreen elements so that you can easily navigate and activate elements when you are ready to play audio files or view videos and DVDs.

Title Bar
Displays the name of the program.

Menu Bar
Displays menus which, when clicked, reveal commands for managing your multimedia items.

Quick Access Box
When clicked, this box displays a menu of other playlists and media sources you can select to play.

Features Taskbar
The left side of the window lists tab links to key features.

Playback Controls
Use these buttons to control how a video or music file plays and to make adjustments to the sounds.

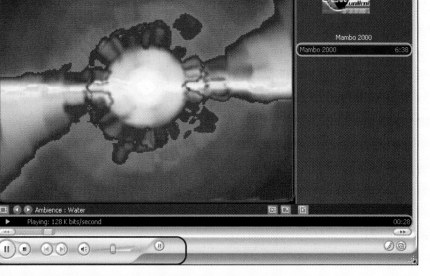

Playlist Pane
Displays the individual tracks of a CD or DVD, or any song names in a customized playlist.

Video/Visualization Pane
Displays the current video, or in the case of audio, displays visualizations or information about the song.

Media Information Pane
Displays a subset of information about the current content, such as the album art and title.

You can change the
size of the Windows
Media Player window
to free up space on
your desktop. For
example, you can
switch to Skin, or
Compact, mode to
reduce the Windows
Media Player window
to a smaller size that
displays a graphical
theme.

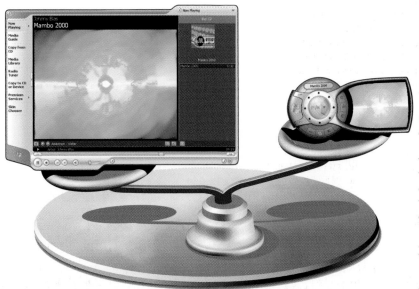

Skin mode does
not offer access to
all Windows Media
Player features,
but it offers a
convenient way to
listen to music in
the background as
you work with
other programs on
your computer. You
can switch back to
Full mode to
access all the
Windows Media
Player features
again.

CHANGE THE PLAYER WINDOW SIZE

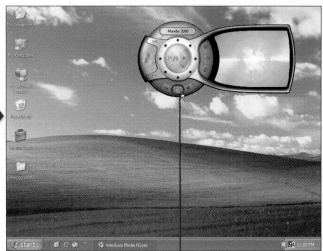

1 Click the **Switch to Skin Mode** button (⊚).

■ The Windows Media
Player window switches to
Skin mode.

■ You can drag the Skin
mode window to where you
want it on the desktop.

2 Click the **Return to Full Mode** button (▦).

■ The Windows Media
Player window switches
back to Full mode.

DISPLAY OR HIDE THE FEATURES TASKBAR

When working in Full mode, you can customize the Windows Media Player window by hiding or displaying the Features taskbar. You can free up more viewing space in the Video/Visualization pane by hiding the features tabs.

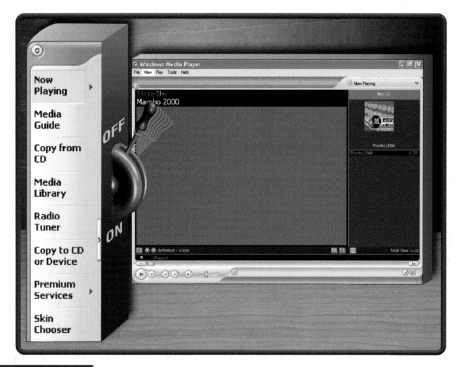

DISPLAY OR HIDE THE FEATURES TASKBAR

1 Click **View**.

2 Click **Full Mode Options**.

3 Click **Hide Taskbar**.

■ You can also click the **Hide Taskbar** button (⊙).

■ Windows Media Player hides the Features taskbar.

4 Click the **Show Taskbar** button (⊙) to view the tabs again.

CUSTOMIZE THE NOW PLAYING PAGE

You can customize the Now
Playing page in Windows
Media Player by hiding or
displaying various features.
By default, all of the
features appear on the
page. You can hide items
that you do not want to
view, or hide features
that you are not currently
using. For example, you
can hide the Playlist pane
to view more of the Video/
Visualization pane.

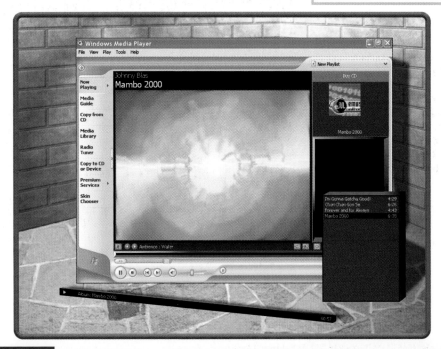

CUSTOMIZE THE NOW PLAYING PAGE

1 Click the **Now Playing**
features tab.

2 Click **View**.

3 Click **Now Playing
Options**.

4 Click the feature that you
want to hide.

■ A checkmark appears
next to the name of active
features. No checkmark
indicates the feature is
hidden.

■ Windows Media Player
hides the feature.

■ In this example, the
Playlist pane is no longer
visible onscreen.

CHANGE INTERFACE SKINS

When you use Windows Media Player in Skin mode, you can choose from a variety of graphical themes to give the Windows Media Player window a unique appearance. A *skin* is simply an interface that controls the appearance of the Windows Media Player window and its features.

Windows Media Player offers you a selection of over 20 skins. You can also download more skins from the Windows Media Web site. See the section "Download a New Skin" to learn more.

CHANGE INTERFACE SKINS

1 Click the **Skin Chooser** tab.

Note: You must switch to Full mode to view the feature tabs. See the section "Change the Player Window Size" to learn more about switching modes.

2 Click a skin to view an example of the interface.

3 When you have selected the skin that you want, click **Apply Skin**.

■ Windows Media Player switches to Skin mode and displays the skin you selected.

■ You can click here to return to Full mode again.

DELETE A SKIN

You can delete a skin that you no longer want to use with Windows Media Player. For example, you may want to delete a skin that you downloaded from the Internet but decide that you do not want to use. Once you delete a skin, it is permanently removed from the Skin Chooser list.

DELETE A SKIN

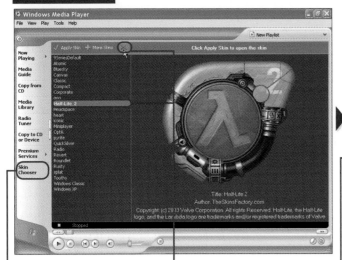

1 Click the **Skin Chooser** tab.

Note: You must switch to Full mode to view the feature tabs. See the section "Change the Player Window Size" to learn more about switching modes.

2 Click the skin that you want to remove.

3 Click the **Delete Selected Skin** button ▨.

■ The Confirm Skin Delete dialog box appears.

4 Click **Yes**.

■ Windows Media Player removes the skin.

DOWNLOAD A NEW SKIN

You can download new skins to use with Windows Media Player from the Windows Media Web site. The site displays a variety of skins, and when you find one that you want to use, it installs automatically after you download it.

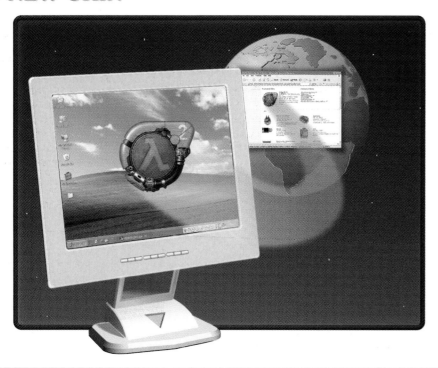

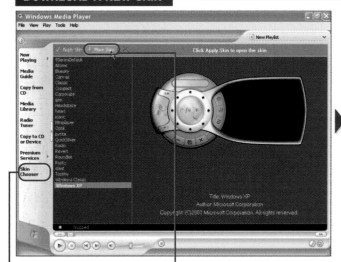

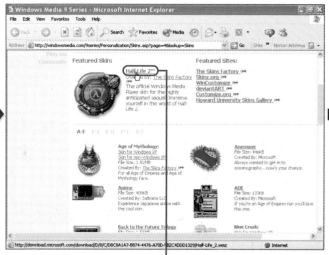

1 Click the **Skin Chooser** tab.

Note: You must switch to Full mode to view the feature tabs. See the section "Change the Player Window Size" to learn more about switching modes.

2 Click **More Skins**.

■ Your Web browser opens to the Windows Media Web site page, which displays a collection of downloadable skins.

Note: You may need to log onto your Internet connection before accessing the Web page.

3 Click the link for the skin you want to download.

I tried several skins and they do not offer the same buttons. Why not?

The playback and other options buttons available on a skin are determined by the developer who created the skin. Many of the skins available on the Windows Media Web site are created by third-party developers, so the options contained in each skin vary. You can easily find missing options by right-clicking over the skin to access a shortcut menu of Windows Media Player window controls.

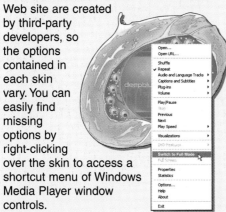

Where can I find more Windows Media Player skins?

The Windows Media Web site offers links to other sites where you can download player skins. Sites like The Skins Factory (www.theskinsfactory.com), Skinz.org (www.skinz.org), and WinCustomize (www.wincustomize.com) offer a lot of skins for you to try. You can also conduct a Web search using the keywords "Windows Media Player skins" to locate more sources for skins.

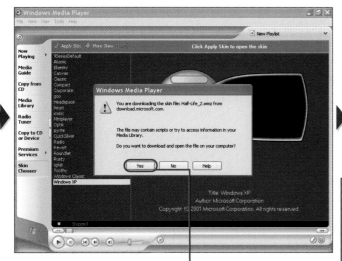

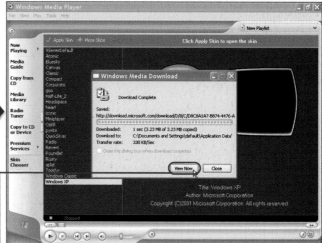

■ A dialog box appears, asking you to confirm that you want to download the skin file.

4 Click **Yes**.

■ The Windows Media Download dialog box appears when the download is complete.

5 Click **View Now**.

■ Windows Media Player displays the new skin.

Note: The Windows Media Web page remains open until you close it. You can close the Web browser window and exit your Internet connection when you finish downloading.

Another way to customize the Full mode in Windows Media Player is to change the interface color. You can choose from a variety of color combinations that change the appearance of the window's interface and features tab.

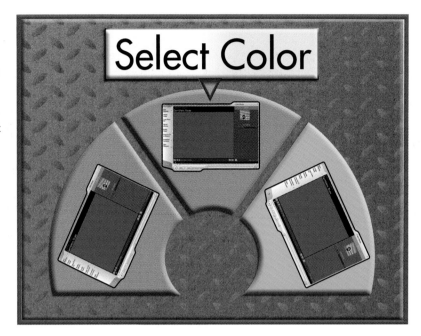

CHANGE INTERFACE COLORS

1 Click the **Change Player Color** button (⬚).

Note: You must switch to Full mode to change the interface color. See the section "Change the Player Window Size" to learn more about switching modes.

■ The interface color changes.

2 Click the ⬚ button again to continue cycling through color variations.

CHANGE INTERFACE VISUALIZATIONS

While you listen to music CDs and other audio files in Windows Media Player, you can display colors and shapes that move to the music. Called *visualizations*, the graphical displays appear in the middle of the Windows Media Player window on the Now Playing page in Full mode, or in the view area in Skin mode.

Windows Media Player comes with several visualizations that you can display in the Windows Media Player window. You can also download more visualizations from the Windows Media Web site (www.windowsmedia.com).

CHANGE INTERFACE VISUALIZATIONS

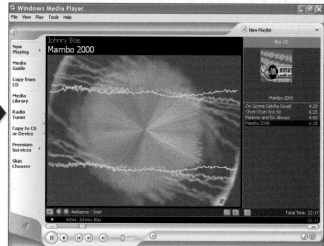

1 Click **View**.

2 Click **Visualizations**.

3 Click a visualization category.

4 Click a visualization.

■ Windows Media Player displays the new visualization.

Note: If the Video/Visualizations pane is not in view, click the Now Playing tab to display the visualization.

ACTIVATE THE MINI PLAYER TOOLBAR

You can use the Mini Player toolbar to perform basic playback functions while the Windows Media Player window is minimized. New to Windows Media Player 9, the Mini Player toolbar is integrated in the Windows desktop taskbar, and offers you shortcuts to common playback features. For example, you can replay a song without displaying the entire Full mode or Skin mode player window.

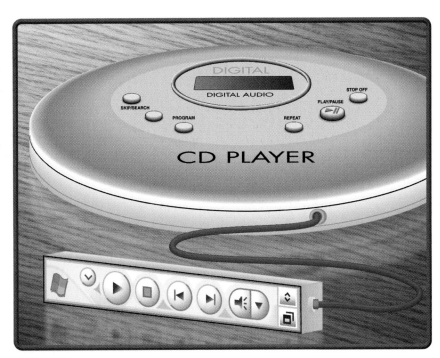

ACTIVATE THE MINI PLAYER TOOLBAR

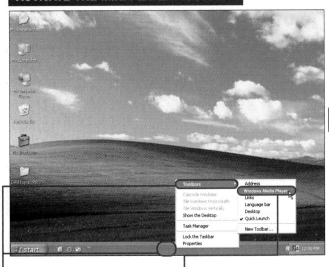

1 Right-click the Windows taskbar.

2 Click **Toolbars**.

3 Click **Windows Media Player**.

■ If a check mark appears next to the feature name, then the toolbar feature is already active.

■ Open the Windows Media Player program window.

4 Click the **Minimize** button ( ).

How do I turn the Mini Player toolbar off?

You can turn off the toolbar feature by right-clicking the taskbar, clicking **Toolbar**, and then deselecting the **Windows Media Player** toolbar. Once the feature is off, you can minimize the program to a regular program window icon on the taskbar instead of the toolbar.

How do I adjust the volume using the Mini Player toolbar?

You can click the **Volume** button ⌄ to display a slider that you can click and drag to adjust your speaker volume for the song currently playing. Click the **Volume** button ⌄ again to hide the Volume slider.

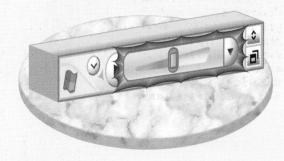

■ The Windows Media Player window closes, and the Mini Player toolbar appears on the taskbar.

■ You can click a playback button to control music or video playback.

■ You can click here to display the Video/Visualization pane.

5 Click the **Restore** button ([🗗]).

■ The Windows Media Player window reappears.

You can adjust the way in which sound and video play in Windows Media Player. For example, you can use the graphic equalizer feature in Windows Media Player to fine-tune your computer's audio playback, such as adjusting the speaker balance. You can also adjust the hue, contrast, or brightness levels for a video that you are viewing.

CHANGE AUDIO AND VIDEO SETTINGS

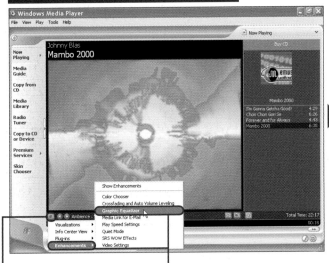

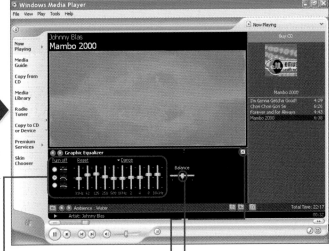

ADJUST AUDIO SETTINGS

1 Click the **Select Now Playing Options** button (▣).

■ You can also click the **View** menu and click **Now Playing Options**.

2 Click **Enhancements**.

3 Click **Graphic Equalizer**.

■ Windows Media Player displays an Enhancements pane below the Video/Visualization pane.

4 Adjust the audio settings.

■ You can drag a slider to adjust a setting.

5 Click the ☒ button.

■ The Enhancements pane closes.

What other Enhancement options can I adjust?

You can click the **Next Controls** ( ) and **Previous Controls** ( ) buttons at the top of the Enhancements pane to scroll through sets of controls other than the graphic equalizer and video settings. Other controls include play speed settings, media links, quiet mode, SRS WOW effects — controls for digitally processed audio effects — a color chooser for the Windows Media Player background, cross-fading, and auto volume leveling.

What do the preset settings do in the graphic equalizer?

Depending on what type of sound file you plan to listen to in Windows Media Player, you can display a distinct set of equalizer presets, such as Rock or Jazz. To access the full preset list, click the **Select Preset** link and choose a preset from the list. The Default preset is selected automatically unless you specify another preset.

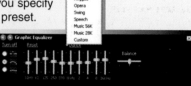

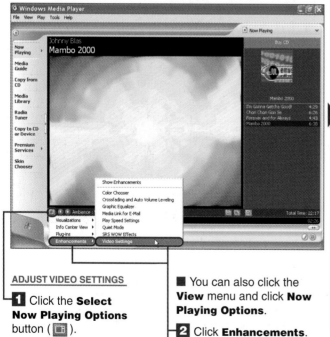

ADJUST VIDEO SETTINGS

1 Click the **Select Now Playing Options** button ( ).

■ You can also click the **View** menu and click **Now Playing Options**.

2 Click **Enhancements**.

3 Click **Video Settings**.

■ Windows Media Player displays the Enhancements pane.

4 Adjust the video settings.

■ You can drag a slider to adjust a setting.

5 Click the ⊠ button.

■ The Enhancements pane closes.

CONFIGURE PLAYER OPTIONS

You can configure additional Windows Media Player settings to further customize the program. For example, you can configure how often Windows Media Player checks for software updates, fine-tune connection speeds for streaming media, and specify privacy settings. You can find all of the Windows Media Player configuration settings in the Options dialog box.

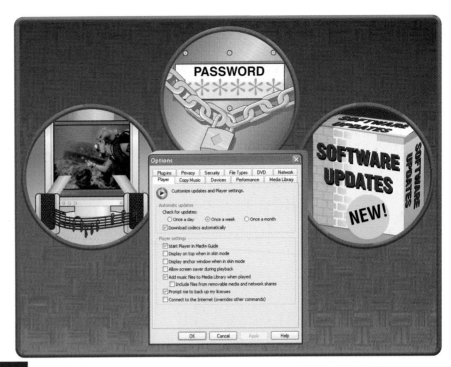

CONFIGURE PLAYER OPTIONS

1 Click **Tools**.

2 Click **Options**.

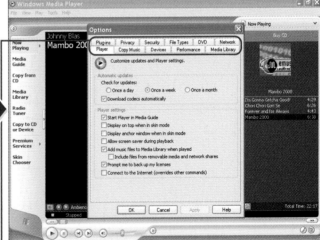

■ The Options dialog box appears.

3 Click a tab for the type of configuration settings you want to adjust.

■ You can find settings for controlling how the program window works on the Player tab.

Can I access the Options dialog box while viewing the Windows Media Player in Skin mode?

Yes. Right-click an empty area of the Windows Media Player window, and then click **Options**.
The Options dialog box appears. The right-click menu offers shortcuts to other common Windows Media Player features and commands, including a command for switching back to Full mode.

How do I set properties for a CD or DVD drive to work with Windows Media Player?

You can configure CD and DVD drives, and portable devices for downloading files and tracks from the Windows Media Player window, using the Devices tab in the Options dialog box. Select the device that you want to configure and then click **Properties**. The Properties dialog box appears for the device, and you can specify settings, such as analog or digital playback, and copy features.

■ You can click the File Types tab to specify which file formats you want to play automatically in the Windows Media Player window.

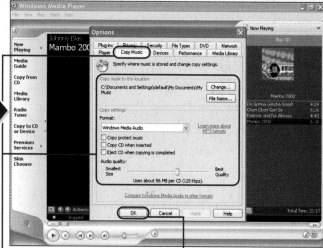

■ You can click the Copy Music tab to specify a location for storing audio files that you copy.

4 Set the configuration options that you want to change.

5 Click **OK**.

■ Windows Media Player applies the new settings.

CHAPTER 7

Playing Audio Files with Windows Media Player

You can listen to your favorite music in Windows Media Player. This chapter shows you how to listen to music CDs, use the playback controls, and create playlists.

PLAY A MUSIC CD

You can play your favorite music CDs in Windows Media Player. The Now Playing page displays the individual tracks on the CD in the Playlist pane, while the Video/Visualization pane pulsates with the musical beats as the CD plays.

PLAY A MUSIC CD

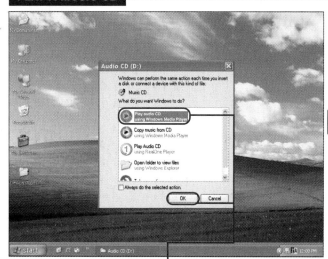

PLAY A CD

1 Insert a CD into your computer's CD-ROM drive.

■ The Audio CD dialog box appears.

Note: See the section "Play an Audio File" later in this chapter to learn how to play audio files that you store on your computer.

2 Click **Play audio CD using Windows Media Player**.

3 Click **OK**.

■ The Windows Media Player window appears, and begins playing the first song.

■ This area displays the current visualization.

Note: See Chapter 6 to learn how to select other visualizations.

■ The playlist displays each song on the CD, along with the song length.

■ The album title appears here.

■ You can drag the **Seek** slider ( ) to play a specific part of a song.

How do I mute a song?

To turn off the sound in Windows Media Player, click the **Mute** button (⊲). The song continues playing, but the sound is muted. Click the button again to turn the sound back on.

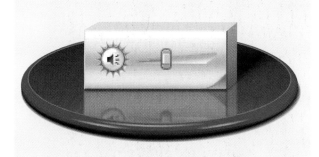

Can I change visualizations during playback?

Yes. You can click the **Previous Visualization** button (◉) or the **Next Visualization** button (◉) to quickly switch between the available visualization schemes in Windows Media Player.

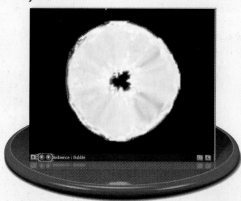

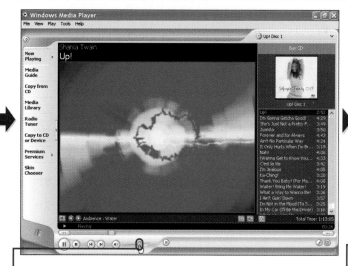

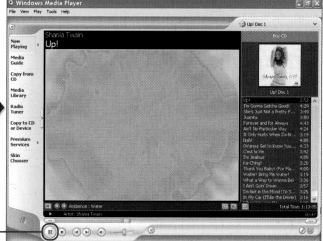

ADJUST THE VOLUME

4 Click and drag the **Volume** slider (▯).

■ Drag the slider left to decrease the volume.

■ Drag the slider right to increase the volume.

PAUSE PLAY

5 Click the **Pause** button (⏸).

■ Windows Media Player pauses playback.

CONTINUED

PLAY A MUSIC CD

You can use the playback buttons at the bottom of the Windows Media Player window to control how a CD plays. For example, you can stop a CD and then select another song to play, or you can pause play if you have to leave the computer.

PLAY A MUSIC CD (CONTINUED)

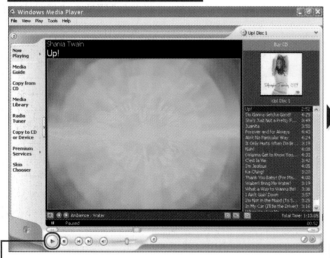

RESUME PLAY

6 Click the **Play** button (▶).

■ Windows Media Player resumes playback where you left off.

STOP PLAY

7 Click the **Stop** button (■).

■ Windows Media Player stops playback.

■ If you click the Play button (▶) after clicking the Stop button (■), then the current song starts over again.

My Playlist pane does not list the song titles. Why not?

When you play a music CD, Windows Media Player tries to gather information about the album encoded in the CD. However, if it cannot ascertain song titles, it displays track numbers instead. To type a song title, select the track number, right-click the track, and click **Edit** from the pop-up menu. Windows Media Player highlights the song in the playlist. Type a song title and press **Enter**.

Can I make the same CD play over and over again?

Yes. Click the **Play** menu, then click **Repeat**. Windows Media Player places a check mark next to the command name to indicate the feature is active. This Repeat command tells Windows Media Player to start playing the album over again. To turn the Repeat feature off again, open the **Play** menu and click **Repeat**.

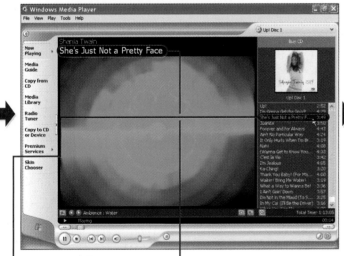

PLAY ANOTHER SONG

8 Double-click the song you want to play in the Playlist pane.

■ Windows Media Player begins playing the song.

■ The current song title appears here.

PLAY SONGS RANDOMLY

9 Click the **Turn Shuffle On** button ( ).

■ Windows Media Player shuffles the order of play.

SKIP A TRACK

You can tell Windows Media Player to skip tracks on a music CD. Skipping tracks allows you to enjoy the songs you like without having to listen to songs you do not want to hear.

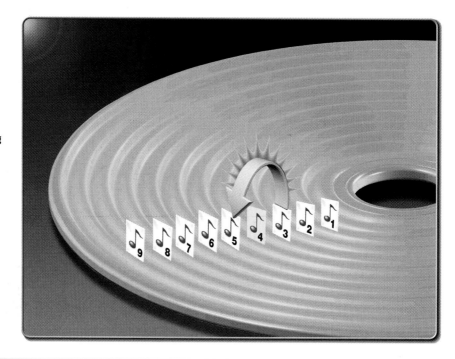

SKIP A TRACK

1 Click the track or tracks that you want to skip.

■ To select multiple tracks, press and hold the **Shift** key while clicking track names.

2 Right-click any track that you want to skip.

3 Click **Disable Selected Tracks**.

■ The track or tracks that you mark for skipping appear dimmed in the playlist.

■ When you play the album, Windows Media Player skips the tracks.

■ To enable the tracks again, select the tracks, right-click, and click **Enable Selected Tracks**.

DISPLAY MUSIC DETAILS

You can use the Info Center view to see details about the album or track that you are currently playing. Instead of viewing the default visualization on the Now Playing page, you can view details about the artist, the album, lyrics, and tag info.

DISPLAY MUSIC DETAILS

1 Click the **Now Playing** tab.

2 Click **View**.

3 Click **Info Center View**.

4 Click a display option for the music details.

■ You can click **Always Show** to always display the information rather than the visualization screen.

■ You can click **Show Only When Detailed Media Information Is Available** if you only want to view details when available.

■ The Video/Visualization pane shows details about the song or album.

■ You can click a tab to view pertinent details.

SPECIFY TRACK ORDER

You can edit a CD playlist to create your own song order. For example, you may want to specify the first song as the last song you listen to, or move a favorite song to the top of the playlist. By default, the Playlist pane lists songs in the order in which they are stored on the music CD.

SPECIFY TRACK ORDER

DRAG AND DROP SONG TITLES

1 Click the song title you want to move.

2 Drag the title up or down in the playlist.

3 Release the mouse button.

■ The song moves to the new location in the track order.

■ Repeat steps **1** to **3** to move other songs.

■ When you play the CD, the tracks play in the new order.

Can I sort my playlist?

Yes. You can sort your playlist by headings, such as artist name, song name, and album. To sort your playlist, click the **Select Playlist Options** button ( ), click **Sort**, and then click a sort order. Windows Media Player sorts the playlist. You can also activate the **Randomize** command to shuffle the tracks in a random order for playback.

Can I hide the Media Information pane to view more of my tracks?

Yes. The Media Information pane above the Playlist pane displays information about the current album. You can hide it by right-clicking the pane and clicking **Show Media Information**. This hides the Media Information pane. To display it again, click the **View** menu, click **Now Playing Options**, and then click **Show Media Information**.

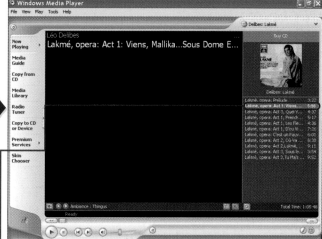

ACTIVATE THE MOVE UP OR MOVE DOWN COMMAND

-**1** Right-click the song title you want to move.

-**2** Click a movement option.

■ You can click **Move Up** to move the song up in the track order.

■ You can click **Move Down** to move the song down in the track order.

└─ ■ The song moves to the new location in the track order.

■ Repeat steps **1** and **2** to move other songs, or to continue moving the same song to another location.

USING THE MEDIA LIBRARY

You can use the Media Library feature in Windows Media Player to manage all of the media files on your computer, including audio files that you listen to with Windows Media Player. The Media Library also enables you to organize links to other digital content, such as music on the Internet.

USING THE MEDIA LIBRARY

SEARCH FOR FILES

1 Click the **Media Library** tab.

2 Click **Tools**.

3 Click **Search for Media Files**.

*Note: The first time you open the Media Library, a dialog box appears, prompting you to search for multimedia files. Click **Yes** to conduct the search automatically.*

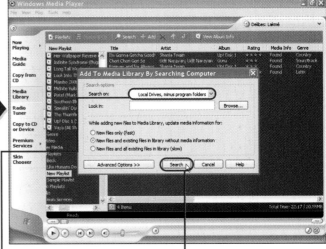

■ The Add To Media Library By Searching Computer dialog box appears.

4 Click ∨ and specify which folder or drive you want to search, or you can search the default selections.

5 Click **Search**.

**My Media Library is quite large.
How do I search for a specific file?**

Click the **Search** button at the top of the
Media Library page. A Search toolbar
appears. Type your search criteria or
keyword and then click **Find Now**. Search
results appear in the Search Results playlist.

**How does the Media Library determine what
category to use for a multimedia file?**

Files are automatically grouped into the
categories based on their media content
information. Media content information, also
called *metadata* or *tags*, includes information
such as the artist name, song title, rating,
play count, and composer. Media content
information also identifies
the file type.

■ A dialog box appears,
displaying the progress of
the search.

─6 When the search is
complete, click **Close**.

VIEW FILES

■ The Contents pane
displays expandable and
collapsible categories for
viewing files in the list.

─7 Click the category ⊞
icon to expand a category.

■ You can click the category
⊟ icon to collapse a
category.

■ The Details pane displays
filenames and information.

─8 Double-click a filename
to play the file.

■ You can drag a border to
resize a pane to display
more or less information.

ADD MUSIC CD TRACKS TO THE MEDIA LIBRARY

You can add tracks from a music CD to the Media Library in Windows Media Player. This allows you to listen to an album without having to put the CD into your CD-ROM drive each time. The process of adding tracks from a CD is called *copying,* or *ripping,* in Windows XP.

The Media Library helps you to organize and manage audio files on your computer. After you add a music track, you can play it from the Media Library page.

ADD MUSIC CD TRACKS TO THE MEDIA LIBRARY

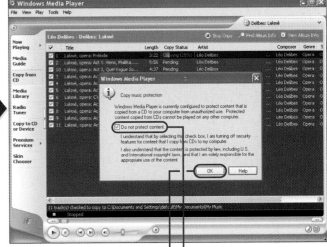

1 Insert a CD into your computer's CD-ROM drive.

2 Click the **Copy from CD** tab.

3 Select the CD tracks that you want to copy.

■ By default, all the tracks are selected for copying. To deselect a track that you do not want to copy, click the check box next to the song title (☑ changes to ☐).

4 Click **Copy Music**.

■ Windows Media Player displays a dialog box the first time you copy a music CD.

■ Click here if you want to play the songs on other computers (☐ changes to ☑).

5 Click **OK**.

How do I remove an item from the Media Library?

Select the file that you want to remove in the Media Library page and then click the **Delete** button (☒). Select a deletion option from the following: **Delete from Playlist**, **Delete from Library**, or **Delete Playlist**. To permanently remove the file from the Media Library, click **Delete from Library**.

Does the Media Library store information about albums that I copy?

Yes. To view album information, first select the album in the Contents pane of the Media Library page. Then, click the **View Album Information** button (▣). The Details pane displays any detailed album information that is available.

■ Windows Media Player begins copying the track or tracks.

■ The Copy Status column displays the copy progress.

■ After each file is copied, the Copy Status column displays a Copied to Library message.

PLAY AN AUDIO FILE

Windows Media Player can play audio files that you store on your computer. The Media Library lists all of the audio files that you save to your hard drive. When you select an audio file from the Media Library list and play it in Windows Media Player, you can also switch to the Now Playing page to view a visualization along with the song.

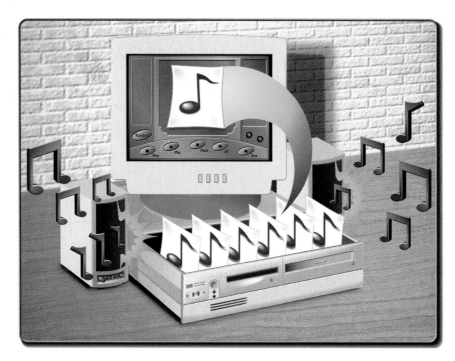

PLAY AN AUDIO FILE

1 Click the **Media Library** tab.

2 Open the folder containing the audio file that you want to play.

3 Click the audio filename.

Note: See the section "Using the Media Library" to learn more about expanding and collapsing categories and viewing files.

4 Click the **Play** button (▸).

■ Windows Media Player begins playing the audio file.

■ You can click the **Now Playing** tab to view a visualization with the song.

■ You can use the playback buttons to control how the song plays.

RATE A SONG

To help you keep track
of which songs and
music tracks you like
the best, you can apply
your own ratings in the
Media Library. Windows
Media Player's rating
system allows you to
assign anywhere from
one to five stars to an
audio file that you store
in the Media Library.

RATE A SONG

■1 Click the **Media Library**
tab.

■2 Click the song that you
want to rate.

■3 Right-click the Rating
column.

■4 Click **Rate Selected
Items**.

■5 Click a rating.

■ Windows Media Player
applies the new rating.

CREATE A PLAYLIST

A *playlist* is a collection of songs, or music tracks, copied from a music CD, stored on your computer hard drive, or downloaded from the Internet. You can create customized playlists in Windows Media Player that play only the songs that you want to hear.

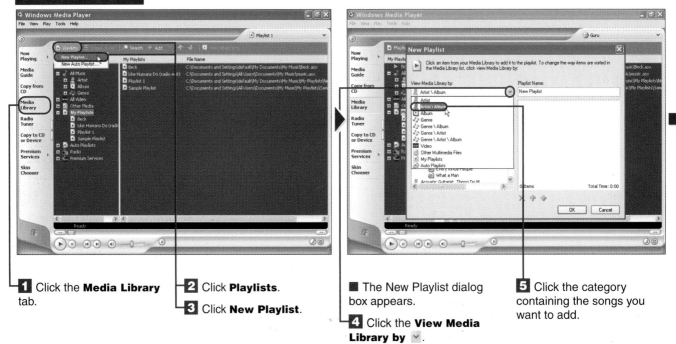

1 Click the **Media Library** tab.

2 Click **Playlists**.

3 Click **New Playlist**.

■ The New Playlist dialog box appears.

4 Click the **View Media Library by** ⌄.

5 Click the category containing the songs you want to add.

Can I add items to a playlist?

Yes. Right-click the item that you want to add in the Media Library page, and click **Add to Playlist**. The Add to Playlist dialog box appears. Click the playlist to which you want to add the item and click **OK**.

What does the Queue-It-Up button do?

You can use the Queue-It-Up button () to temporarily add entire albums, artist lists, and other playlists to a playlist. While playing the playlist, click the **Media Library** tab, click the item that you want to add, and then click the **Queue-It-Up** button ().

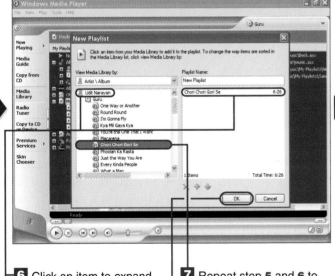

6 Click an item to expand it, and select the song you want to add.

■ Windows Media Player adds the song to the playlist.

7 Repeat step **5** and **6** to add more songs to the playlist.

8 When you finish creating the list, click **OK**.

■ Windows Media Player adds the playlist to the My Playlists category in the Media Library.

9 Click the playlist name to highlight it.

10 Click the playlist name again to edit the name.

11 Type a new name for the list.

12 Press **Enter**.

■ Windows Media Player saves the new name.

PLAY A PLAYLIST

You can quickly access a custom playlist or any other playlist that you save in the Media Library. When you play a playlist, you can use the Windows Media Player's playback features to control how the music plays, and you can view a visualization on the Now Playing page.

PLAY A PLAYLIST

1 Click the **Media Library** tab.

2 Click the **My Playlists** category.

3 Click a playlist.

4 Click the **Play** button (▶).

■ You can also start a playlist using the Quick Access drop-down menu.

■ Windows Media Player begins playing the list.

■ You can click the **Now Playing** tab to display the Video/Visualization pane and the Playlist pane.

■ To rename the list, you can click the list name twice, type a new name, and press **Enter** to save your changes.

DELETE A PLAYLIST

You can remove a playlist
that you no longer want
to keep in the Media
Library. For example,
you can delete a playlist
that you do not use
anymore, or delete an
auto playlist created by
Windows Media Player.

DELETE A PLAYLIST

1 Click the **Media Library**
tab.

2 Click the **My Playlists**
category.

3 Click the playlist you
want to delete.

4 Click the **Delete**
button (■).

5 Click **Delete Playlist**.

■ A dialog box appears,
warning you that you are
about to delete a file.

6 Click a deletion option
(○ changes to ◉).

■ You can choose **Delete
from Media Library only** to
remove the playlist from the
library.

■ You can choose **Delete
from Media Library
and my computer** to
permanently remove
the playlist.

7 Click **OK**.

■ Windows Media Player
removes the playlist from the
Media Library.

EDIT A PLAYLIST

You can edit the playlists that you create in a variety of ways. For example, you can use the Edit Playlists dialog box to rearrange the order of songs or music tracks, add additional songs, and remove songs you no longer want to include in the list.

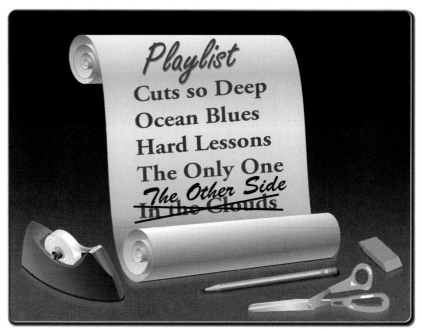

EDIT A PLAYLIST

ADD A SONG

1 Click the **Media Library** tab.

2 Click the playlist you want to modify.

3 Click **Playlists**.

4 Click **Edit Playlist**.

■ You can also edit a playlist directly in the Media Library by using the controls at the top of the page.

■ The Edit Playlist dialog box appears.

5 To add a song to the list, expand the category to display the song, then click the song title.

■ Windows Media Player adds the song to the playlist.

What are auto playlists?

The Media Library can generate its own playlists, called *auto playlists*, based on criteria that you specify. Predefined auto playlists appear under the Auto Playlist category in the Media Library's Contents pane. To create a new auto playlist, click the **Playlists** button and then click **New Auto Playlist.** The New Auto Playlist dialog box appears. Type a name for the list, and define the list criteria by clicking the icons and selecting criteria. Click criteria links to further define the criteria. Any files that meet the criteria are automatically added to the auto playlist. You can play auto playlists just like regular playlists.

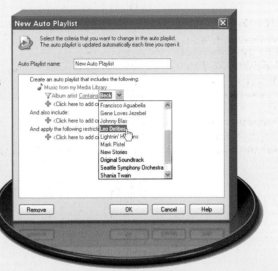

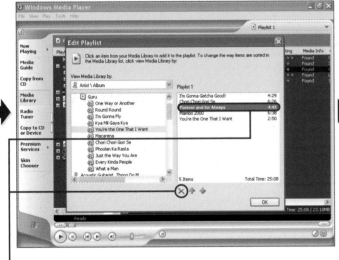

REMOVE A SONG

6 To remove an item from the playlist, click the item.

7 Click ☒.

■ Windows Media Player removes the song from the playlist.

CHANGE THE PLAYLIST ORDER

8 To change the playlist song order, select a song you want to move.

9 Click a direction arrow to reposition the item in the list.

■ Click 🔼 to move an item up the list.

■ Click 🔽 to move an item down the list.

10 When you finish editing the list, click **OK**.

■ Windows Media Player saves your changes to the playlist.

USING THE MEDIA GUIDE

You can use the Media Guide page in Windows Media Player to access the latest music, movie links, and news on the Internet. The Media Guide is actually a Web page that updates regularly with new information and links. You can use the page to download and listen to audio and video files.

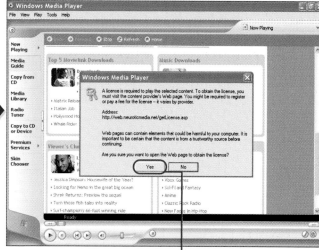

1 Click the **Media Guide** tab.

Note: You must connect to the Internet in order to view the Media Guide Web page.

2 Click a link.

■ The Media Guide may display another Web page with more links to explore.

■ A dialog box may appear, prompting you to obtain a license to play the song.

■ To obtain a license, you may have to register or pay a fee to listen to the song.

3 Click **Yes** to acquire a license.

When I click an audio link, a Media Bar Settings dialog box appears. What should I do?

The Media Bar Settings dialog box asks if you want to play the audio or video file from within the Internet Explorer Web browser window. Click **No** to listen to or view the file in Windows Media Player instead.

How do I navigate the Media Guide pages?

You can click the **Back** ( ) and **Forward** ( ) buttons at the top of the Media Guide page to navigate between pages. You can click the **Home** button ( ) to return to the home page — the page that first appears when you click the Media Guide tab. You can click the **Refresh** button ( ) to refresh a page's content. You can click the **Stop** button ( ) to stop loading a page.

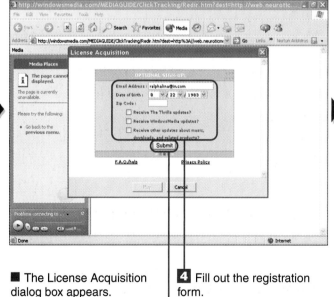

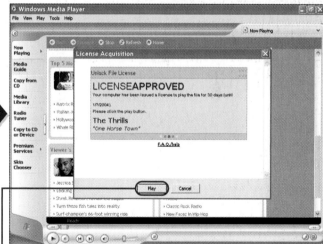

■ The License Acquisition dialog box appears.

4 Fill out the registration form.

5 Click **Submit**.

6 Click **Play**.

■ Windows Media Player begins playing the song.

■ You can close any additional Web pages that appear and click the **Now Playing** tab in Windows Media Player to listen to the song.

■ Windows Media Player adds the downloaded song to the Media Library, where you can play it anytime.

CHAPTER 8

Playing Music from the My Music Folder

You can access and manage your music files using the My Music folder. Windows XP automatically creates the My Music folder and stores it in the My Documents folder. This chapter shows you how to listen to and manage audio files from within the My Music folder.

You can quickly access your digital audio files using the My Music folder. By default, Windows XP creates the My Music folder inside the My Documents folder. The My Music folder not only stores your music files, but also includes links to quickly access common tasks.

You can create subfolders within My Music to further organize digital audio files. For example, you can create one folder for favorite songs and another for sound effects.

OPEN THE MY MUSIC FOLDER

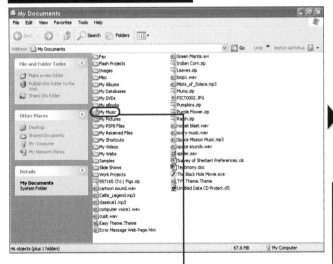

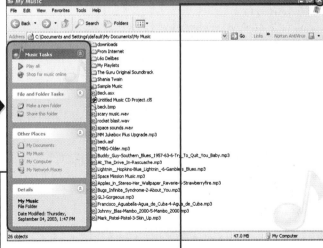

1 Open the My Documents or My Computer window.

2 Double-click the **My Music** folder.

■ The My Music folder window appears.

■ A list of links to common tasks appears in the left pane of the folder window.

■ To close the folder window at any time, click ⊠.

You can use the My Music folder to keep track of your digital audio files. The folder window includes a toolbar for navigating folders on your computer as well as a pane of links to common commands. Take a moment to become familiar with the folder window elements.

Title Bar
Displays the name of the open folder.

Menu Bar
Displays menus which, when clicked, reveal commands for managing your files and folders.

Standard Buttons
Displays shortcut buttons to common tasks, such as navigating between folders and changing folder views.

Address Bar
You can go directly to a folder and file if you type the path in this bar and click the Go button.

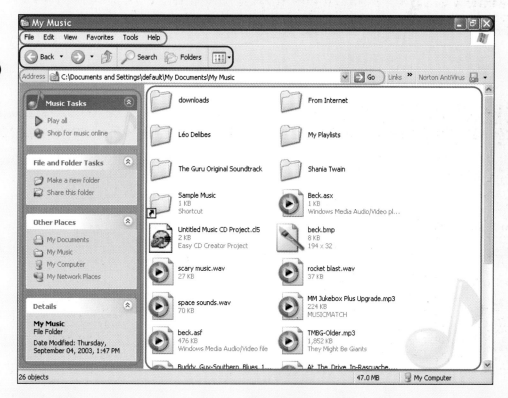

Task Pane
The left side of the folder window lists links to common tasks, folders, and details about your files.

List Box
Displays a listing of the folders and files within the current folder. You can change the way in which items are listed in this box.

PLAY MUSIC FILES

You can play a music file from the My Music folder. The folder window's Task pane features a playback control that you can activate. When you activate this control, the Windows Media Player opens and starts playing the music file.

The Play All or Play Selection links are only available in the My Music folder window or folders that you create with the My Music template. Other folders that you create in the My Documents main folder do not feature this shortcut.

PLAY MUSIC FILES

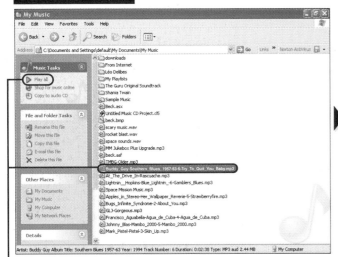

PLAY ALL THE FILES

1 Click the file that you want to play in the My Music folder.

2 Click the **Play all** link.

■ To play multiple files, press and hold the `Shift` key while selecting files. The **Play all** option becomes the **Play selection** option. Click **Play selection** to play the files.

■ Windows Media Player opens and plays all the files in the My Music folder, starting with the file you selected.

Note: See Chapter 7 to learn more about playing music files in Windows Media Player.

Can I play an entire album?

Yes. You can store songs from a single music CD or album in a single folder within the My Music folder. To play all the songs within a folder, simply click the folder name and then click **Play Selection** in the Task pane. Windows Media Player then plays the entire album.

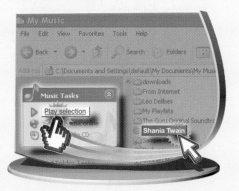

If I play all the music files in the My Music folder, can I add songs from other folders to the playlist?

Yes. After activating the **Play All** link in the My Music folder, Windows Media Player treats all the songs in the folder as a playlist. You can add other songs from other folders, such as subfolders within the My Music folder, to the playlist. To do so, open the folder containing the song you want to add, right-click the filename, and then click **Queue-It-Up**. Windows Media Player immediately adds the song to the bottom of the playlist.

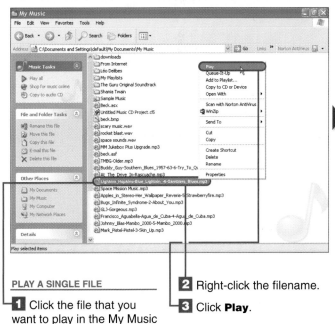

PLAY A SINGLE FILE

1 Click the file that you want to play in the My Music folder.

2 Right-click the filename.

3 Click **Play**.

■ Windows Media Player opens and plays the file.

Note: See Chapter 7 to learn more about playing music files in Windows Media Player.

DISPLAY AUDIO FILE DETAILS

You can use the Details view in the My Music folder window to view details about your audio files. You can also control the number of detail columns that appear in the list box. By default, when you view audio files in the Details view, eight columns appear in the list box area to describe the audio files. You can add details to or remove details from the listings, using the Choose Details feature.

DISPLAY AUDIO FILE DETAILS

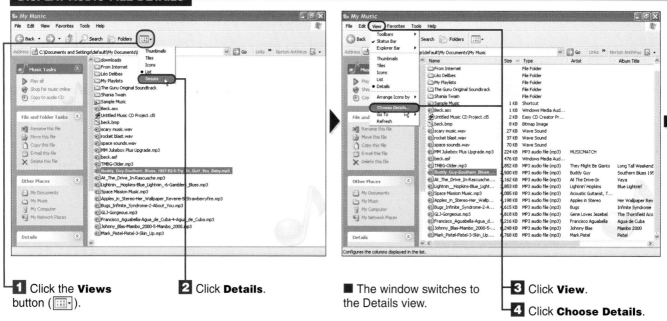

1 Click the **Views** button (▦▾).

2 Click **Details**.

■ The window switches to the Details view.

3 Click **View**.

4 Click **Choose Details**.

Which view is best for working with audio files?

Out of five possible views, the Details, List, and Tiles views work best for examining audio files in the My Music folder. The Details view lists details about the files in columnar format. The List view simply lists the files by name. The Tiles view displays names along with file size information. To change your view at any time, simply click the button and select another view.

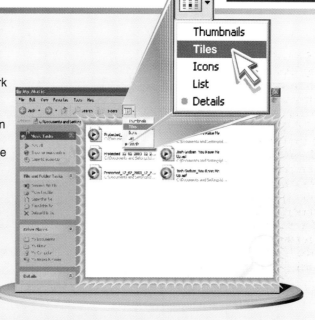

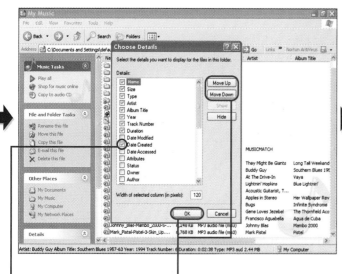

■ The Choose Details dialog box appears.

5 Select the columns that you want to appear in the Details view (☐ changes to ☑).

■ You can deselect columns that you want to hide in the Details view (☑ changes to ☐).

■ You can click these buttons to change the order of selected columns.

6 Click **OK**.

■ The list box reflects your changes.

DELETE A MUSIC FILE

You can remove a music file or any other type of audio file you no longer want. After removing the file from the My Music folder or a subfolder, Windows XP places the file into the Recycle Bin. You can permanently remove the file at a later time.

See your Windows XP documentation to learn more about using the Recycle Bin.

DELETE A MUSIC FILE

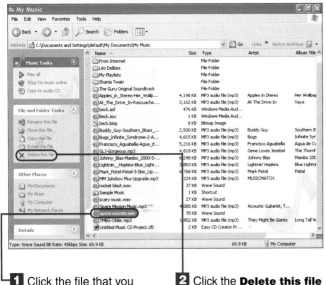

1 Click the file that you want to remove.

2 Click the **Delete this file** link.

■ A Confirm File Delete dialog box appears.

3 Click **Yes** to continue with the deletion.

■ You can click **No** to cancel the deletion.

■ Windows XP removes the file from the folder and places it in the Recycle Bin.

OPEN A MUSIC FILE IN ANOTHER PLAYER

If you have other media-player programs installed on your computer, you can open a specific player to play a song in the My Music Folder. For example, you may prefer playing a particular audio file in a program other than Windows Media Player.

OPEN A MUSIC FILE IN ANOTHER PLAYER

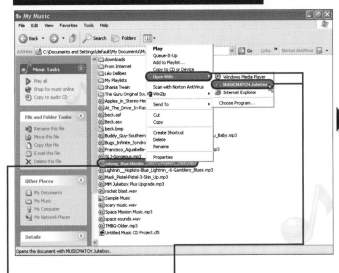

1 Right-click the file you want to play.

2 Click **Open With**.

3 Click the player you want to use.

■ The player program opens and plays the song.

■ This example uses Musicmatch Jukebox to play the file.

ADD A MUSIC FILE TO A PLAYLIST

You can add a music file from the My Music folder to a playlist that you store and play with Windows Media Player. Playlists allow you greater control over which songs you listen to and in which order they play.

See Chapter 7 to learn more about working with playlists in Windows Media Player.

ADD A MUSIC FILE TO A PLAYLIST

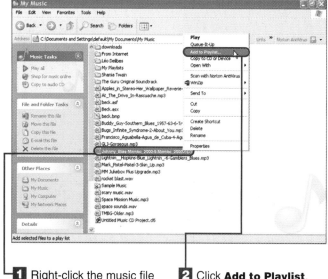

1 Right-click the music file you want to add.

2 Click **Add to Playlist**.

■ Windows Media Player opens automatically, and the Add to Playlist dialog box appears.

3 Click the playlist to which you want to add the file.

4 Click **OK**.

■ Windows Media Player adds the music file to the end of the selected playlist.

SET VOLUME CONTROLS

You can control the
volume of your computer's
speakers using the Volume
Control dialog box. For
example, if the volume of
the music file you play in
the My Music folder is too
low, you can adjust the
volume to a higher level.

SET VOLUME CONTROLS

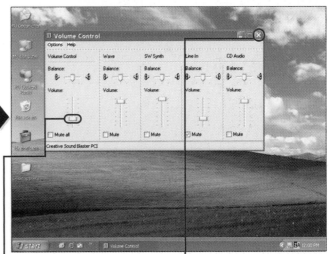

1 Double-click the Volume
icon in the system tray.

■ The Volume Control dialog
box appears.

2 Make any adjustments
to the volume settings by
dragging sliders up or down.

3 Click ☒ to exit the dialog
box and apply the changes.

SHARE A MUSIC FILE ON YOUR COMPUTER

You can share your music files with others who use your computer. When you copy a music file to the Shared Documents folder, the file is available to other users who log into the computer with a different login.

SHARE A MUSIC FILE ON YOUR COMPUTER

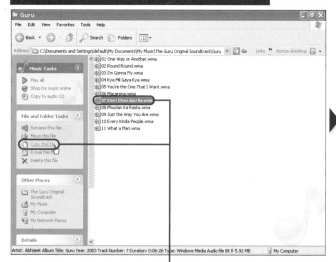

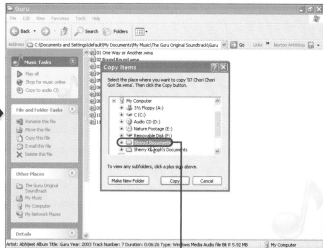

COPY THE MUSIC FILE

1 Open the folder containing the music file you want to share.

2 Click the music file.

3 Click the **Copy this file** link.

■ The Copy Items dialog box appears.

4 Click the **Shared Documents** folder to expand the contents.

Can I share playlists as well as music files?

Yes. You can copy a playlist to the My Music subfolder that resides within the Shared Documents folder to share the list with other users. By default, Windows Media Player playlists are stored in the My Playlists subfolder, located within the My Music folder. Playlists are stored in the WPL file format. See Chapter 7 to learn more about playlists.

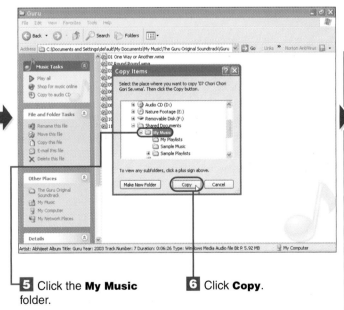

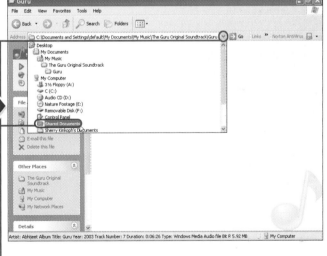

5 Click the **My Music** folder.

6 Click **Copy**.

VIEW THE SHARED DOCUMENTS FOLDER

7 Click ⌄.

8 Click **Shared Documents**.

■ Windows XP opens the Shared Documents folder view, allowing you to open the My Music folder and view the copied file.

E-MAIL A MUSIC FILE

You can e-mail any music that you store in the My Music folder. The folder window includes a special task link that connects you to your default e-mail program for sending a file.

E-MAIL A MUSIC FILE

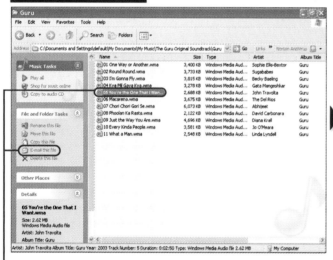

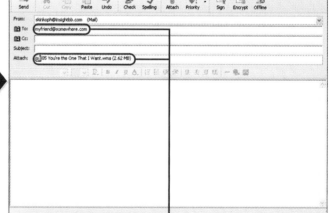

1 Click the music file that you want to e-mail.

2 Click the **E-mail this file** link.

Note: If you want to send a large audio file, then you may need to use a compression program to compress the file before sending.

■ Outlook Express opens a message window for you.

Note: If you use another program as your default e-mail editor, it may open instead of Outlook Express.

■ The music file appears as a file attachment.

3 Type the e-mail address of the person to whom you want to send the file.

Can I send more than one file at a time?

Yes. To select multiple files in the My Music folder, press and hold the **Shift** key while clicking the filenames. If the files are not contiguous, then you can press and hold the **Ctrl** key while clicking the filenames. You can also use the **Ctrl** key technique to select files from different folders.

My friend sent me a music file attachment. How do I add it to the My Music folder?

Right-click the file attachment and click **Save As**. When the Save Attachment As dialog box appears, navigate to the My Music folder, open a subfolder in which you want to save the file, and then click **Save**.

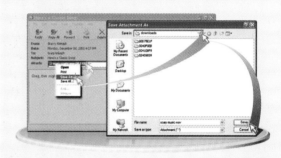

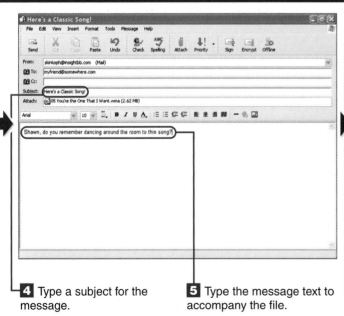

4 Type a subject for the message.

5 Type the message text to accompany the file.

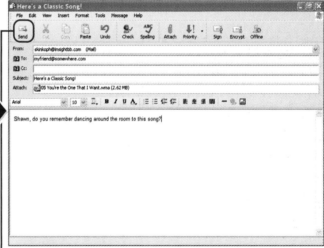

6 Click the **Send** button (⬛).

■ Outlook Express sends your message and file.

Note: If you are not currently connected to the Internet, Windows may prompt you to log in to your Internet account.

SEARCH FOR AN AUDIO CLIP

You can use the Windows XP Search tools to help you locate audio clips and other music files on your computer. For example, you can search for a specific name or file type.

FILE TYPE:
☐ Picture ☑ Music ☐ Video
All or part of filename:
Guitar

SEARCH FOR AN AUDIO CLIP

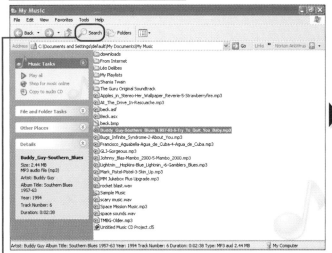

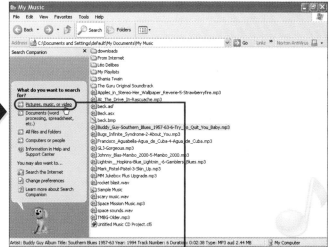

1 Click the **Search** button (🔍 Search).

■ The Search tasks pane appear.

2 Click the **Pictures, music, or video** link.

What advanced search options can I use?

If you click **Use advanced search options** in the Search pane, then you can display additional options for defining a search. For example, you can tell Windows XP to search for a file in a particular drive or folder, or to search for files of a certain size or modification date. Click the icon to expand the options for each category. You can also find more search options if you click **More advanced options**.

Use advanced search options

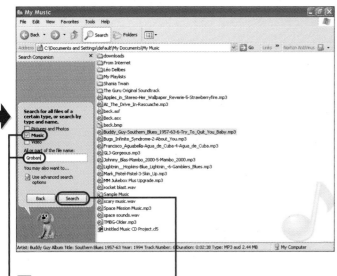

3 Click the **Music** check box (☐ changes to ☑).

4 Type the name of the file that you want to find.

■ To search for a particular file format without knowing the name of the file, type an asterisk followed by a period and the file extension, such as ***.mp3**.

5 Click **Search**.

■ Windows XP searches for the file and displays the search results in the list box area.

COPY MUSIC FROM OTHER ALBUM FOLDERS

By default, when you copy music CDs onto your computer, Windows XP stores the songs from a single album in its own folder. You can combine albums into folders to create larger collections of songs. You can also copy songs from one folder to another to create a new playlist.

COPY MUSIC FROM OTHER ALBUM FOLDERS

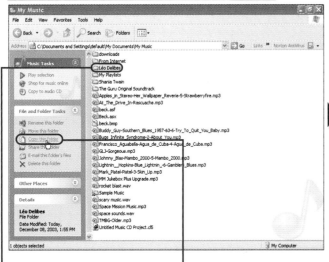

1 Click the album folder that you want to copy.

2 Click the **Copy this folder** link.

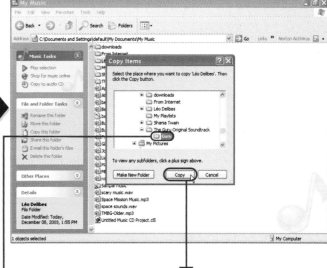

■ The Copy Items dialog box appears.

3 Click the folder to which you want to copy the album.

4 Click **Copy**.

■ Windows XP copies the album into the designated folder.

DISPLAY ALBUM ART

You can view album
cover art within the My
Music folder window. If
Windows XP copies art
information when you
copy songs from a music
CD, you can use the
Thumbnails view of the
folder window to view
the album art.

DISPLAY ALBUM ART

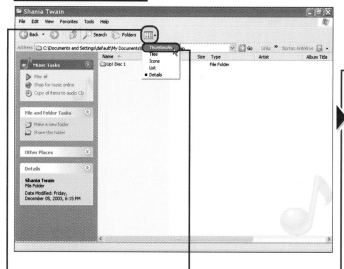

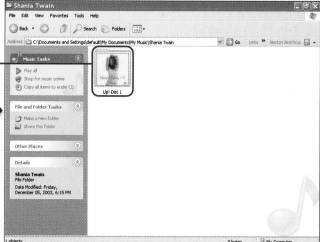

1 Click the **Views**
button (▦▾).

2 Click **Thumbnails**.

■ The folder icon displays
the album cover art.

CHAPTER 9

Downloading and Recording Audio Files

Windows XP lets you create your own CDs and shop for digital music online. This chapter shows you how to download and record audio files using Windows XP.

UNDERSTANDING DIGITAL MEDIA DELIVERY AND RECORDING METHODS

The world of digital media includes many technical terms and concepts that you need to understand. If you are new to digital media, then take a moment to learn about the basic concepts behind audio downloading and recording. Understanding these concepts can help you make better use of the Windows XP multimedia features.

Streaming Media

Digital media that plays while it downloads to your computer is called *streaming media*. Although streaming media does not take up space on your computer — unless you choose to save it — it does require your computer's processing power and a good Internet connection. Streaming media is an efficient method of delivering audio and video files across the Internet or a network and is a popular way to listen to music online or view Web movies and animations.

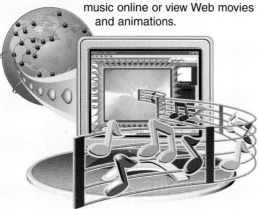

Buffering

When you download streaming media, Windows XP stores it in a temporary buffer or storage area. For example, when playing a streaming audio file in Windows Media Player, the program sends a portion of data to your computer before any content starts playing. If your Internet connection experiences gaps in the download process, information from the buffer can help smooth the playback. Heavy Internet traffic can cause noticeable interruptions in your streaming media.

Licenses

Illegal music and video file distribution is a growing concern on the Internet. To help prevent illegal distribution, companies offer digital licenses to legal users. A license merely defines how the end user is allowed to use a media file. A license can specify how often you can copy the file to a portable device, such as a portable MP3 or WMA player, or to a CD. A license can also limit the number of copies you can make of the file, as well as how many times you can play it back on your computer. Some licenses are only good for a short amount of time, while others are unlimited.

Tracking Licenses

When you download music from the Internet, the license downloads with the music file. To keep your licenses safe, it is a good idea to back them up on a CD or floppy disk in case you ever lose the original. If a license expires or cannot be located, you can no longer play the associated file.

Ripping CDs

When you copy files from a music CD to your computer, the copying process is called *ripping*. You can rip songs from various sources to create unique playlists in Windows Media Player. The copying process involves encoding the data from the CD to your hard drive. To copy music, you need only your computer and a CD drive. During the copying process, you can convert the files to a particular file format for use on your computer, such as MP3 or WMA.

Burning CDs

When you copy files from your computer to a blank CD or DVD, the encoding process is called *burning*. To burn music CDs, you need a CD-RW drive and a blank CD. You can also burn videos to a DVD-RW drive. If your computer has a CD/DVD burner, then you can burn both music and videos. You can burn music tracks copied from another music CD or tracks that you download from the Internet. You can use Windows Media Player to burn to the CD-R (recordable) or CD-RW (rewritable) formats. You can only record on CD-Rs once, while you can rewrite on CD-RWs multiple times.

SHOP FOR MUSIC ONLINE

Windows XP offers you two ways to shop for music through your computer. You can shop for music CDs from the My Music folder window, or you can shop for music using the Media Guide page. Either method requires that you connect to the Internet.

SHOP FOR MUSIC ONLINE

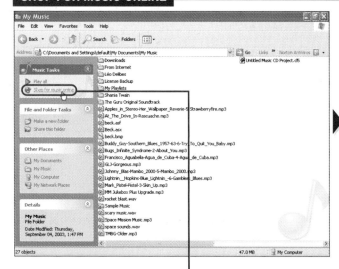

SHOP IN THE MY MUSIC FOLDER

1 Open the **My Music** folder.

2 Click the **Shop for music online** link.

■ Your Web browser opens to the online shopping page of the Windows Media Web site.

■ You can click a link to buy a CD from an online merchant.

■ You can look up other artists and albums by typing keywords here.

Can I buy a digital music CD online?

Yes. There are numerous Web sites that let you purchase and download entire digital albums or select songs from an album. For example, the Liquid Audio Web site (http://store.liquid.com) offers sample WMA music files that you can listen to in Windows Media Player before you buy, as well as entire digital music albums that you can purchase and download. Conduct a Web search with the keywords "digital music downloads" to see a variety of Web sites that you can browse through for digital albums. See the next section to learn how to use subscription services to buy digital music.

**SHOP IN WINDOWS
MEDIA PLAYER**

1 Launch Windows Media Player.

2 Click the **Media Guide** tab.

3 Click **Music**.

4 Click an artist link.

■ A page appears with links for ordering music online.

USING ONLINE SUBSCRIPTION SERVICES

You can use the Premium Services feature in Windows Media Player to purchase and subscribe to digital music and video services. Once you subscribe to a service such as MusicNow or Napster, you can download and stream media in Windows Media Player, for a monthly fee.

USING ONLINE SUBSCRIPTION SERVICES

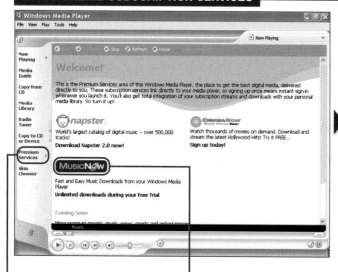

1 Launch Windows Media Player.

2 Click the **Premium Services** tab.

3 Click a service that you want to use.

■ A Web page appears for the service in Windows Media Player.

Note: You must connect to the Internet before signing up for an online subscription service.

4 Follow the links to sign up for the service.

Downloading and Recording Audio Files **9**

Do any services have trial offers?

Yes. Some subscription services, like MusicNow, have a free trial offer. For a designated amount of time you can try the service before you buy it. To find more trial offers, perform a Web search for digital music services.

Can I cancel my subscription?

Yes. If you lose interest in your subscription, find that you do not use it enough, or perhaps the site does not offer the variety of music that you want, then you are free to cancel your subscription. Be sure to check out the site's rules and guidelines for use and cancellation steps.

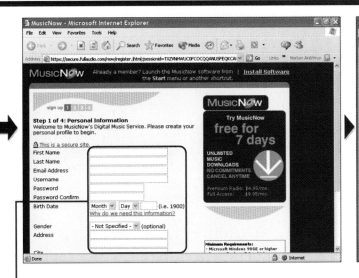

■ When you sign up for the service, you are required to register for an account.

5 Type in the appropriate registration information.

■ The type and amount of information required may vary between services.

■ After you sign up for a service, you can start downloading music files onto your computer.

Note: Some subscription services require you to install software as a part of purchasing the service.

■ The next time you click the Premium Services tab, Windows Media Player connects you to the service, and you can search for and download audio files.

171

DOWNLOAD A MUSIC FILE FROM THE WEB

When you click a free music download, you can save it to a folder on your computer's hard drive. When you play the file, Windows Media Player opens and plays the song.

Some music files that you download from the Internet include licenses granting you permission to use the file. You may have to fill out a registration form before completing the download to acquire a license. Be sure to read your license carefully to know your limitations on file usage.

DOWNLOAD A MUSIC FILE FROM THE WEB

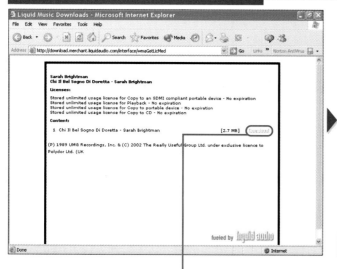

1 Navigate to the Web page containing the music file link you want to download.

2 Click the **Download** link.

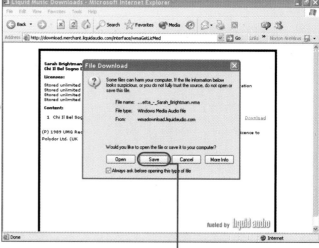

■ The File Download dialog box appears.

3 Click **Save**.

Can I download directly to a portable device?

Yes. As long as the device is installed and connected to your computer, you can use the Save As dialog box to direct your download to the portable device. You may prefer to download the file to your computer's hard drive to keep the original file, then burn a copy of the file to the device later using Windows Media Player's Copy to CD or Device feature. You can learn more about burning files to CDs later in this chapter.

■ The Save As dialog box appears.

■ You can click here to save the file to another folder or drive.

4 Click **Save**.

■ Windows XP starts downloading the file.

■ The process may take a few seconds or a few minutes, depending on the speed of your Internet connection.

■ When the download is complete, the Download complete dialog box appears.

5 Click **Close**.

■ You can continue downloading other files, or open Windows Media Player to listen to the newly downloaded file.

Note: See Chapter 7 to learn how to listen to audio files in Windows Media Player.

BACK UP YOUR LICENSES

Many music files that you download from the Internet include licenses. A license grants you permission to save and play the file on your computer. Some licenses allow you to copy the file to other devices or computers. Be sure to back up your licenses frequently.

By default, Windows Media Player backs up your licenses in a default folder, labeled License Backup, within the My Music folder. For added safety, consider backing up your licenses to a CD or floppy disk in case of a computer crash.

BACK UP YOUR LICENSES

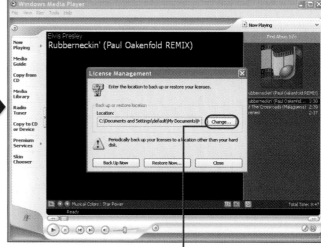

1 Launch Windows Media Player.

2 Click **Tools**.

3 Click **License Management**.

■ The License Management dialog box appears.

4 Insert a CD or floppy disk to which you want to copy the license data.

5 Click **Change**.

How do I know if a file has a license?

To view license information in Windows
Media Player, right-click the filename in
the Media Library and click **Properties**.
The Properties dialog box appears. Click
the **License** tab to determine whether or
not the file has a license. You can use this
same technique to view license information
from the My Music folder.

How do I restore a license?

Reopen the License Management dialog
box in Windows Media Player, and insert
the disk containing the license or locate
the appropriate folder on your hard drive.
Click the **Restore Now** button to begin
restoring the license.

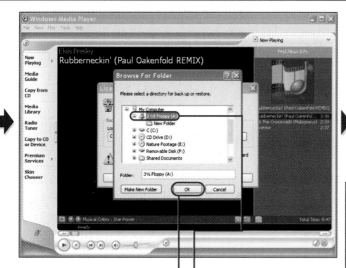

■ The Browse For Folder
dialog box appears.

6 Navigate to the drive to
which you want to copy the
licenses.

7 Click **OK**.

■ The Browse For Folder
dialog box closes.

8 Click **Back Up Now**.

■ Windows Media Player
copies your licenses to the
backup location.

SET AUDIO QUALITY AND FORMAT

Before you begin copying or ripping audio tracks to or from a CD or a computer, you can tell Windows XP what file format to use, copy-protect the files, and specify an audio quality level. If you use Windows Media Player to copy music CD files, the Options dialog box offers controls for audio quality and format.

To learn how to copy music CDs to your computer, see chapter 7.

SET AUDIO QUALITY AND FORMAT

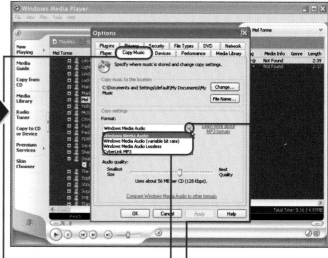

1 Launch Windows Media Player.

Note: See Chapter 6 to learn more about using Windows Media Player.

2 Click **Tools**.

3 Click **Options**.

■ The Options dialog box appears.

4 Click the **Copy Music** tab.

5 Click the **Format** ▾.

6 Click a file format.

Note: Unless you install the MP3 Creation Pack, you may be limited to the WMA format.

Can I copy-protect my files?

Yes. You can select the **Copy protect music** option in the Options dialog box to copy-protect music files that you copy onto your computer. Protected files require a license in order to play them back. You can copy-protect your files if you worry about accidentally using them on another computer illegally.

How can I activate the CD controls, and what do they do?

You can select the **Copy CD when inserted** checkbox in the Copy Music tab of the Options dialog box to tell Windows Media Player to automatically place copied music files in the Media Library when you copy music CDs. You can select the **Eject CD when copying is completed** option if you want to immediately eject the CD when you are finished copying.

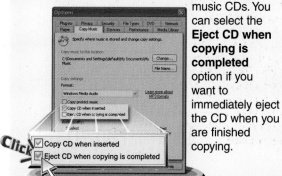

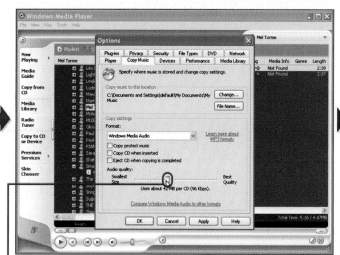

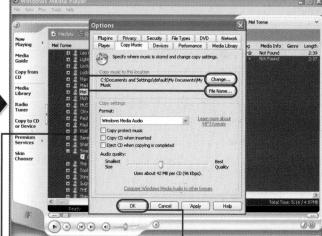

7 Click and drag the Audio quality slider to set a bit rate for the files that you are copying.

■ Drag the slider to the left to create smaller files with lower sound quality.

■ Drag the slider to the right to create larger files with higher sound quality.

■ Click the **Change** button to change the default location for files that you copy.

■ If you want to change the information that appears with track names, click the **File Name** button to select items.

8 Click **OK**.

■ Windows Media Player applies the new settings.

BURN MUSIC FILES TO A CD

You can copy, or *burn*, music files from your computer onto a CD. Burning CDs is a great way to create customized CDs that you can listen to on the computer or in a portable device. You can burn music files from within the Windows Media Player window.

To copy music CDs to your computer, see chapter 7.

BURN MUSIC FILES TO A CD

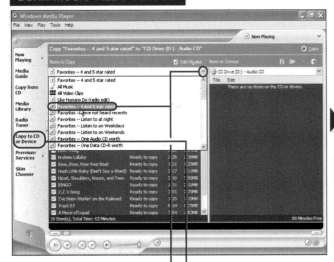

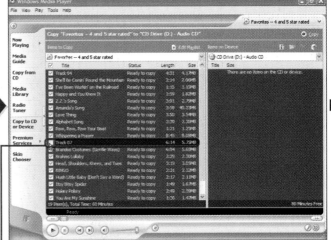

1 Insert a blank CD into your computer's CD-RW drive.

2 Launch Windows Media Player.

Note: See Chapter 6 to learn more about using Windows Media Player.

3 Click the **Copy to CD or Device** tab.

4 Click the **Playlists** ⌄.

5 Click the playlist that you want to copy.

■ Windows Media Player displays the songs.

6 Click to deselect any songs that you do not want to burn to the CD (☑ changes to ☐).

■ By default, Windows Media Player selects all the songs on the playlist for copying.

Can I burn files from the My Music folder?

Yes. Select the tracks that you want to copy from your computer to the music CD, and click the **Copy to audio CD** link in the Music Tasks pane of the My Music folder window. When you activate this link, the Windows Media Player window appears, and you can use the Copy to CD or Device tab to copy the files.

My computer installed with another CD-burning program. Can I use it instead?

Yes. Although Windows Media Player is good for recording WMA file types, there are other good burner programs for creating CDs for MP3 files. For example, Easy CD Creator (www.roxio.com) and NeroMIX (www.ahead.de) are two very popular audio-burning programs you can use. Check your CD-burning documentation to see if it contains the options and features that match what you want to do.

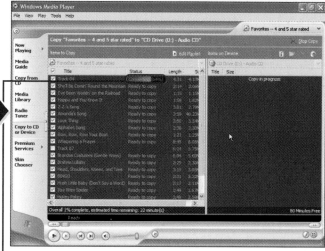

7 Click ⌄.

8 Click the CD drive to which you want to copy.

9 Click **Copy**.

■ Windows Media Player converts the files to CDA format and copies them to the CD.

RECORD YOUR OWN SOUNDS

Windows XP includes a program for recording your own audio, such as narrations and sound effects. As long as your computer has a sound card, speakers, and a microphone, you can record your own sound files.

By default, you can only save sounds that you record with Sound Recorder in the WAV file format.

RECORD YOUR OWN SOUNDS

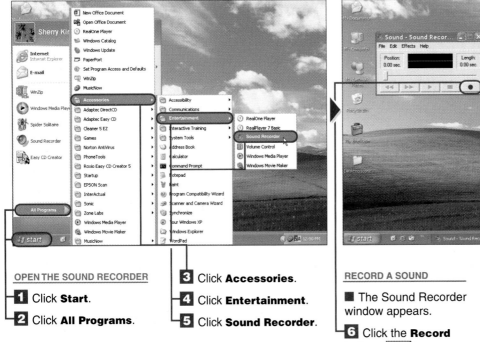

OPEN THE SOUND RECORDER

1 Click **Start**.

2 Click **All Programs**.

3 Click **Accessories**.

4 Click **Entertainment**.

5 Click **Sound Recorder**.

RECORD A SOUND

■ The Sound Recorder window appears.

6 Click the **Record** button (●).

7 Begin speaking into your microphone or creating the sound you want to record.

Can I add any special sound effects with Sound Recorder?

Yes. Click the **Effects** menu in the Sound Recorder window to view effects. You can click the **Add Echo** command to add an echo. You can click the **Reverse** effect to play a sound in reverse. You can also click the **Increase Speed** and **Decrease Speed** commands to distort the sound.

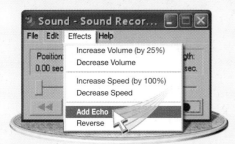

Can I mix sounds?

Yes, you can create overlay effects by combining sounds into a single file. Drag the slider to where you want to overlay a new sound. Then click the **Edit** button and click **Mix with File**. The Mix with File dialog box appears. Select a sound file and click **Open**. Sound Recorder overlays the new sound with the existing sound.

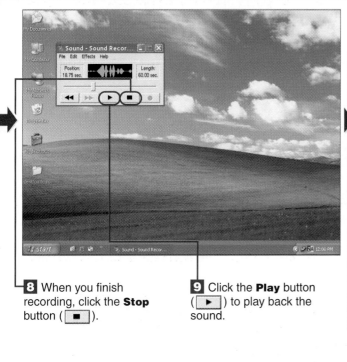

8 When you finish recording, click the **Stop** button (■).

9 Click the **Play** button (▶) to play back the sound.

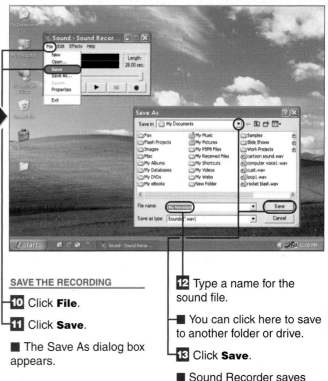

SAVE THE RECORDING

10 Click **File**.

11 Click **Save**.

■ The Save As dialog box appears.

12 Type a name for the sound file.

■ You can click here to save to another folder or drive.

13 Click **Save**.

■ Sound Recorder saves the sound file.

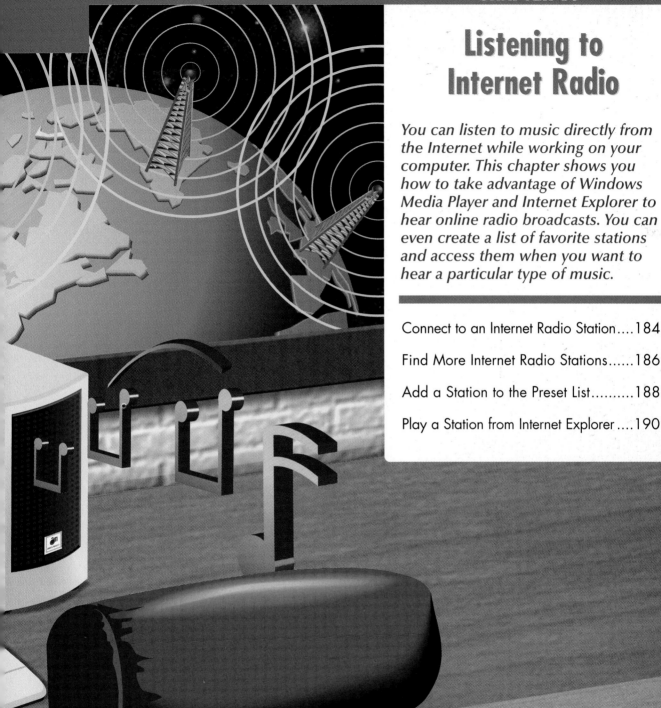

CHAPTER 10

Listening to Internet Radio

You can listen to music directly from the Internet while working on your computer. This chapter shows you how to take advantage of Windows Media Player and Internet Explorer to hear online radio broadcasts. You can even create a list of favorite stations and access them when you want to hear a particular type of music.

CONNECT TO AN INTERNET RADIO STATION

You can quickly tune into an Internet radio station using Windows Media Player. The player includes a variety of *preset channels* or *stations*, which are links to featured radio stations. You can find links to classical, jazz, rock, and talk radio stations.

To listen to an online radio station, you must first log onto your Internet connection and be using a computer with sound capabilities.

CONNECT TO AN INTERNET RADIO STATION

1 Open the Windows Media Player.

Note: See Chapter 6 to learn more about using Windows Media Player.

2 Click the **Radio Tuner** link.

■ Windows Media Player opens the Radio Tuner page and lists featured stations.

3 Click a station to which you want to listen.

I do not see a Play link. How do I play the station?

You can click the **Visit Website to Play** link to visit the station's Web site and listen to the station through your Web browser. You can find a link to play the station on the station's Web site. Some stations require additional information from you before allowing you to listen to the broadcast.

How do I adjust the volume?

You can either click the **Mute** button (◀) to mute the broadcast, or click and drag the **Volume** slider (▯) to increase or decrease the volume. If the volume is too quiet with ▯ at its maximum setting, consider raising the volume with the controls on your computer speakers themselves.

■ Windows Media Player displays a description of the station and several links.

4 Click the **Play** link.

Note: If the featured station does not offer a Play link, see the tip above.

■ Windows Media Player connects you to the station and starts playing.

■ This area of the window displays connecting information.

■ A browser window may also appear and display more information about the station.

■ You can click the **Stop** button (●) to stop receiving the broadcast.

5 To finish listening to the station and exit the Windows Media Player window, click ✕.

FIND MORE INTERNET RADIO STATIONS

You can use the Windows Media Player window to search for additional Internet Radio Stations. Windows Media Player's search categories include everything from country music to news and talk radio broadcasts.

FIND MORE INTERNET RADIO STATIONS

■1 Click the station category that interests you.

Note: See Chapter 6 to learn more about using Windows Media Player.

■ Windows Media Player displays a page of search results.

■ The station's connection speed appears in this column.

■ The station's location appears in this column.

■2 Click a station to which you want to listen.

Can I search by keywords?

Yes. If you still cannot find a station you like, try searching by keyword. Follow these steps:

1 In the Windows Media Player window, click in the **Search** box and type the keywords you want to search for.

2 Click the **Search** button (→).

■ Windows Media Player displays a page of stations that match your search criteria.

3 Click the **Play** link.

*Note: If the featured station does not offer a Play link, you can click the **Visit Website** link and listen to the station using your Web browser.*

■ Windows Media Player connects you to the station and starts playing.

■ A browser window may also open and display more information about the station.

4 When you finish listening to the station, click ☒ to exit the Windows Media Player window.

ADD A STATION TO THE PRESET LIST

You can add your own favorite radio stations to Windows Media Player and tune into them whenever you like. The Windows Media Player window includes a My Stations list that you can use to store links to your favorite stations.

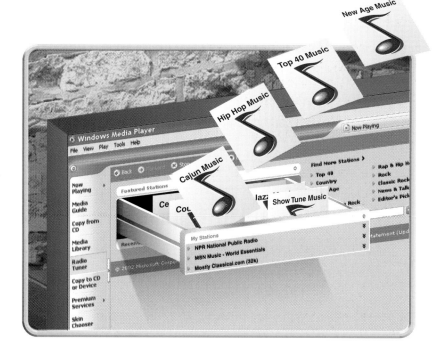

ADD A STATION TO THE PRESET LIST

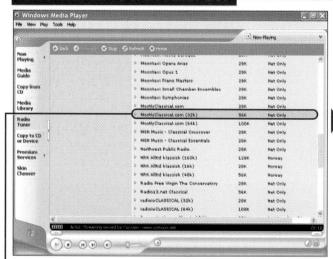

1 Locate the station you want to add to your list.

■ You can add a station from the featured list to your favorites, or you can conduct a search and add stations you find to the list.

Note: See the previous section to learn more about searching for stations.

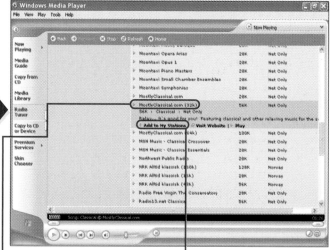

2 Click the station name.

3 Click the **Add to My Stations** link.

How do I remove a station from the My Stations list?

Windows Media Player makes it easy to remove stations from your list of favorite stations. To make edits to your list, follow these steps:

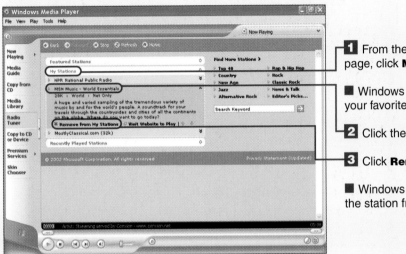

1 From the Radio Tuner home page, click **My Stations**.

■ Windows Media Player lists your favorite stations.

2 Click the station you want to remove.

3 Click **Remove from My Stations**.

■ Windows Media Player deletes the station from your list.

■ Windows Media Player adds the station to your My Stations list.

4 Click the **Home** button.

■ Windows Media Player displays the Radio Tuner's home page.

5 Click **My Stations**.

■ Windows Media Player displays the list with the newly added station.

■ You can click a station to listen to it.

Note: See the section "Connect to an Internet Radio Station" to learn how to listen to a broadcast.

PLAY A STATION FROM INTERNET EXPLORER

You can use the Internet Explorer browser window to play online broadcasts. Using the built-in Media bar, you can choose from a list of stations or search for more stations. When you connect to a station, the Media bar downloads the streaming broadcast.

PLAY A STATION FROM INTERNET EXPLORER

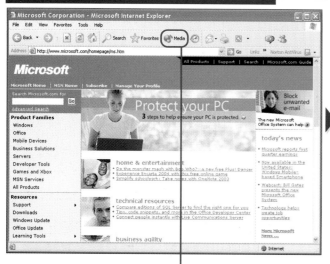

1 Open the Internet Explorer browser window.

2 Click the **Media** button (Media).

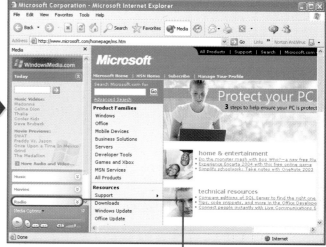

■ The Media bar opens on the left side of the Internet Explorer window.

3 Click **Radio**.

Can I play a station directly from a Web page without the Media bar?

Yes. If a link is available, you can click it to open the appropriate media player. Some Web pages featuring live broadcasts may offer you several links to specify which type of media you want to use to listen to the broadcast. When you make your selection, the appropriate media player opens.

Can I browse other pages while listening to the current station?

Yes. You can continue browsing Web pages with the current broadcast still playing. You can also close the Media bar and continue listening to the broadcast. If you close Internet Explorer or select another station to play, however, the current broadcast stops.

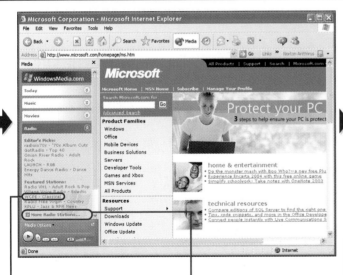

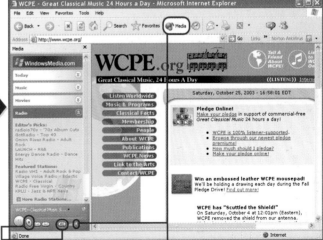

4 Click a station to which you want to listen.

■ To search for additional stations, click here to open an MSN Web page with links to more online stations.

■ The broadcast begins playing.

■ You can click the **Stop** button (⊙) to stop the broadcast.

■ You can click the **Mute** button (⊡) to mute the volume.

■ You can click and drag the Volume slider (⏷) to adjust the volume.

5 Click ⏵ Media to close the Media bar and stop listening to the broadcast.

CHAPTER 11

Playing DVDs with Windows Media Player

If your computer has a DVD drive, you can use it to watch movies and other interactive programs using Windows Media Player. You can view commercial DVDs as well as those you create.

PLAY A DVD

You can use Windows Media Player to play DVDs. If you have a DVD driver and decoder software, you can use the Windows Media Player window to watch any multimedia items stored on a DVD, such as movies and video footage.

Depending on how you set up your DVD drive and Windows Media Player, your DVD may begin playing as soon as you insert it. If not, you can follow the steps in this section to initiate playback.

PLAY A DVD

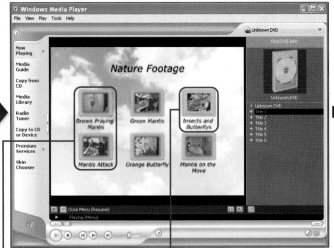

1 Insert a DVD into your computer's DVD drive.

2 Launch the Windows Media Player.

Note: See Chapter 6 to learn more about using Windows Media Player.

3 Click **Play**.

4 Click **DVD, VCD, or CD Audio**.

5 Click your DVD drive's name.

■ Windows Media Player begins to play the DVD and displays the built-in menu.

■ DVD menu items can vary in appearance and can use different layouts.

6 Click the menu item or feature you want to play.

My DVD does not play. Why is this?

Unfortunately, Windows Media Player does not include any DVD decoder software. If you experience trouble playing a DVD, you may need to purchase a DVD decoder pack add-in to add playback capability to Windows Media Player for your particular DVD drive. To search for a decoder plug-in, follow these steps:

4 Click the **DVD Decoder Plug-ins** link.

■ You can read more about available plug-ins and find links to sites that sell the plug-ins, along with instructions for purchasing and downloading them

1 In the Windows Media Player window, click **View**.

2 Click **Plug-ins**.

3 Click **Download Plug-ins**.

■ Your browser window opens and displays a list of plug-in categories for the Windows Media Player.

■ Windows Media Player begins playback.

■ The tracks appear in the Playlist pane.

■ Information about the DVD—if available—appears here, and in the case of commercial DVDs, the cover image also appears.

Note: See the section "Change Screen View Modes" to enlarge the viewing area.

7 When you finish watching the DVD, click ✕ to exit the Windows Media Player window.

You can control how a DVD plays by using the various navigation controls in the Windows Media Player window. The window includes volume and playback controls. You can also navigate to different scenes using the list of tracks in the Playlist pane. All scenes, or tracks, stem from a root menu that directs you to the DVD's contents.

NAVIGATE A DVD

STOP AND START A DVD

1 Click the **Stop** button (▪).

■ Windows Media Player stops the DVD playback.

2 Click the **Play** button (▸).

■ Windows Media Player restarts the playback from the beginning.

■ You can also click the **Pause** button (▮▮) to pause the playback if you want to resume playing in the same scene.

NAVIGATE SCENES

1 Click the **Previous** button (◂).

■ Windows Media Player jumps you to the previous scene.

2 Click the **Next** button (▸).

■ Windows Media Player jumps you to the next scene.

■ You can also navigate directly to a scene in the playlist by double-clicking the scene you want to play.

What is a root menu?

The root menu is the opening menu of a DVD, typically displaying links to the various segments, features, or clips on the DVD. You can return to the root menu at any time to access other elements on the DVD. You can quickly access the root menu with a shortcut menu. Right-click the DVD screen, click **DVD Features**, and then click **Root Menu**.

Can I adjust the DVD's play speed?

Yes. You can choose from three settings: Slow, Normal, or Fast. The slow setting plays the DVD in slow motion. The normal setting plays the DVD at normal speed. The fast setting accelerates the play. To change the play speed, click **Play**, click **Play Speed**, and then select a speed. Windows Media Player selects the normal setting by default.

RETURN TO THE ROOT MENU

1 Click **View**.

2 Click **DVD Features**.

3 Click **Root Menu**.

■ The DVD's opening menu appears in the Windows Media Player window.

CHANGE SCREEN VIEW MODES

You can control the size of your window view of a DVD in Windows Media Player. For example, you can view a movie using the full-screen mode or you can view smaller sizes, such as 50 percent of the original size. You can also close certain elements, such as hiding the Task pane, to see more of the viewing area.

CHANGE SCREEN VIEW MODES

VIEW FULL SCREEN

1 Click the **View Full Screen** button ( ).

■ To hide only the Playlist pane, you can click the **Maximize the Video and Visualization Pane** button ( ).

■ Windows Media Player closes all the program window elements, except for the top and bottom window bars.

2 Click the **Exit Full Screen** button ( ) to return to the default window viewing size.

Can I hide different elements in the Playlist pane?

Yes. To control which elements appear in the Playlist pane, click **View** and then click **Now Playing Options** to display a list of onscreen items you can display or hide. For example, you can hide the listing of tracks and scenes, or you can hide the media description area.

Can I apply full-screen video settings if my Windows Media Player window is resized or in Skin mode?

You can apply some of the viewing size settings to a resized program window, but if your program window is not fully maximized, you cannot change to Full Screen mode. If you switch to Skin mode, then you can still view a DVD while performing other tasks on the Windows XP desktop. To switch to Skin mode, click **View** and then click **Skin Mode**.

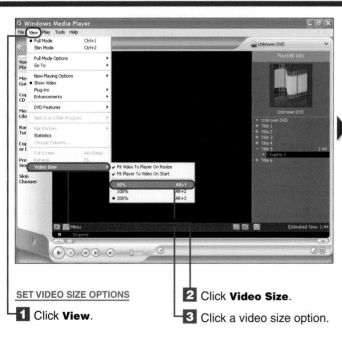

SET VIDEO SIZE OPTIONS

1 Click **View**.

2 Click **Video Size**.

3 Click a video size option.

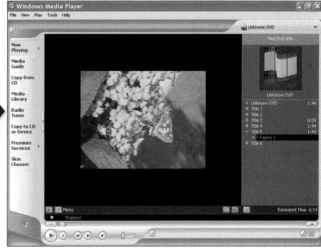

■ Windows Media Player changes the video size.

■ This example changes the video size to 50 percent.

SET ENHANCEMENT OPTIONS

You can activate the Enhancements bar to make adjustments to a DVD's speed, audio, color, and other settings. For example, you can use the Graphic Equalizer enhancement settings to adjust audio channels. After making your adjustments, you can close the Enhancements bar to enlarge the viewing area again.

SET ENHANCEMENT OPTIONS

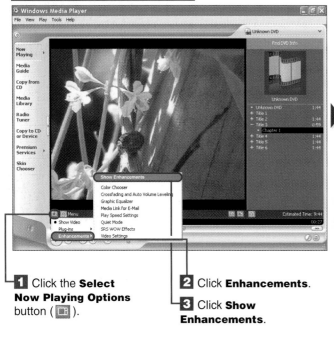

1 Click the **Select Now Playing Options** button ( ).

2 Click **Enhancements**.

3 Click **Show Enhancements**.

■ Windows Media Player displays the Enhancements bar.

■ In this example, the Color Chooser controls appear.

4 Make the changes you want to the option settings.

■ This example enables you to click and drag the Hue or Saturation sliders to change the video color.

5 Click the **Next Controls** button ( ).

Is there a faster way to access the Enhancements settings I want to change?

With the Enhancements bar displaying onscreen, you can right-click the bar and select a specific set of options to view. You can also click the **Select Now Playing Options** button ( ), click **Enhancements**, and then click a set of options.

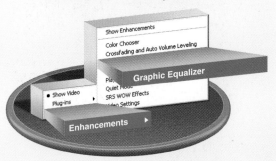

Where can I find additional audio controls?

You can open the Windows Media Player's Options dialog box to find more DVD controls. Click **Tools**, then click **Options** to display the dialog box. Click the **DVD** tab and then click the **Advanced** button to access more audio settings that you can change for playing DVDs.

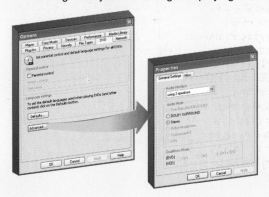

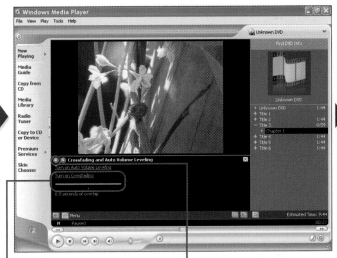

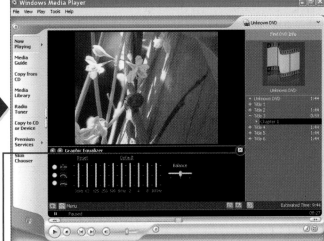

■ The Enhancements bar displays the next set of options.

▄ **6** Make any changes you want to the option settings.

■ You can click the **Previous Controls** button ( ) to return to the previous set of options.

7 When you finish making adjustments, click ⊠.

■ The Enhancements bar closes.

CAPTURE A FRAME IMAGE

You can capture a still frame from your DVD and save it as a picture file. The Windows Media Player includes a command for capturing still frames. When you activate the command, you can save the image as a JPEG or Windows bitmap file. This technique allows you to save an image to use in another project.

CAPTURE A FRAME IMAGE

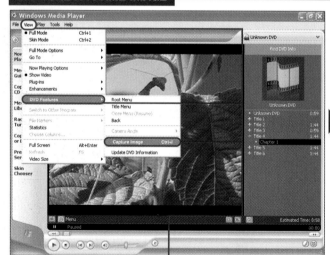

1 Stop or pause the DVD on the frame you want to capture.

Note: See the section "Navigate a DVD" to learn how to stop or pause the playback.

2 Click **View**.

3 Click **DVD Features**.

4 Click **Capture Image**.

■ The Save Captured Image dialog box appears.

5 Select a folder in which you want to store the image.

6 Type a filename.

■ To save the file in a bitmap format instead of the default JPEG format, click here and then click **Windows Bitmap**.

7 Click **Save**.

■ Windows Media Player saves the image.

SET UP LANGUAGE AND SUBTITLE OPTIONS

Many commercial DVDs that you play in Windows Media Player offer other language options. For example, you can view a DVD in French or Spanish. You can switch between available languages as well as display subtitles or closed captioning.

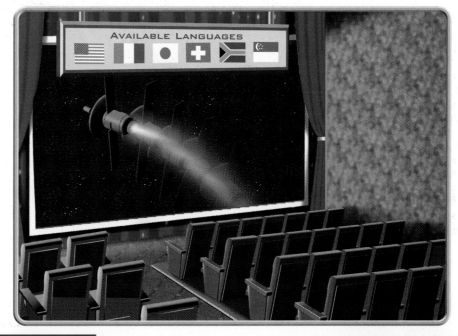

SET UP LANGUAGE AND SUBTITLE OPTIONS

SET A LANGUAGE PREFERENCE

1 Click **Play**.

2 Click **Audio and Language Tracks**.

3 Click a language.

■ Windows Media Player plays the DVD in the language you selected.

SET CAPTIONS

1 Click **Play**.

2 Click **Captions and Subtitles**.

3 Click a titling option.

■ Windows Media Player displays the DVD with the captioning option you selected.

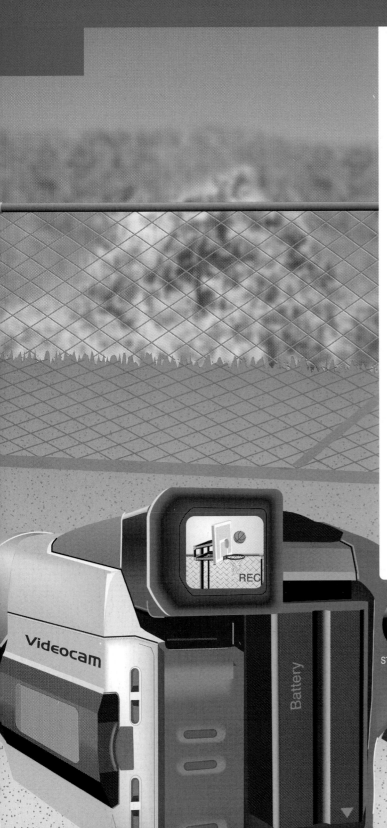

CHAPTER 12

Setting Up Windows Movie Maker

Windows XP includes a program called Windows Movie Maker that lets you capture and edit video footage on your computer. You can turn the footage into a movie file that you can share with others. This chapter shows you how to get started using Windows Movie Maker.

INTRODUCTION TO WINDOWS MOVIE MAKER

Windows XP installs with a program you can use to transfer video footage to your computer. Windows Movie Maker is a video-editing program that you can use to edit video footage that you shoot with a camcorder. With Windows Movie Maker, you can insert transitions between scenes, as well as titles and background music.

System Requirements

To use Windows Movie Maker's basic features, your computer system needs at least a 600 MHz processor, such as a Pentium III, 128MB of RAM, and 2GB of free hard disk space. Your computer system also needs to have a device for inputting audio sources, such as a sound card with microphone or line input jack. For optimal performance, use a minimum 1.4 GHz processor, such as a Pentium 4, and at least 256MB of RAM to improve your use of the program and to edit and view video footage more smoothly on your computer.

Video Sources

There are a variety of video recording devices on the market today, and each source connects to your computer in a different way. Digital video, or DV, camcorders are the latest technology available and allow you to directly download your video footage through an IEEE 1394, or FireWire, connection to your computer. If you have an analog camcorder, you must use a video capture device to connect your video camera to the computer. If you want to download videos from a TV or VCR, you must use a TV tuner card. If you want to record footage from a Web camera, you can use a USB 1 or 2 connection.

Turning Clips into Movies

Windows Movie Maker can help you take video footage that you capture with a video camcorder and turn it into a finished movie. The program includes features for inserting transition effects to control how one scene merges into another, as well as title text and credits. The program also features some video effects that you can use to control how your video images appear in your movie. Windows Movie Maker classifies three types of video footage data that you can work with to create your movies: collections, projects, and movies.

Understanding Collections

A *collection* includes all the elements you import to make a video, such as video clips, audio clips, and photo files. For example, you can download several segments of video footage that you capture on a camcorder, and then import sound effect files, as well as still images. A collection acts as a receptacle for organizing the individual parts of your movie. Items in a collection appear in the Collections pane.

Understanding Projects

As you begin to assemble your video elements, you are creating a project. A *project* contains the timing and sequence of elements in a movie. You add clips to the project's timeline to determine the sequence. You can save a project and return to it later to perform more edits. You save project files with the .mswmm extension.

Understanding Movie Files

After you assemble your movie and insert all the elements, transitions, effects, and titles, you can create a movie file. You can save a movie file on your computer, as an e-mail attachment, or on a DV camera, or record it on a CD. You can save your movie file in the Windows Media Video, or WMV, file format or in the Audio-Video Interleaved, or AVI, file format.

You can launch Windows Movie Maker whenever you are ready to create and work with video clips on your computer. When you finish with the program, you can close it to free up computer memory. If you do not save your work, Windows Movie Maker prompts you to do so before exiting the program window.

OPEN AND CLOSE WINDOWS MOVIE MAKER

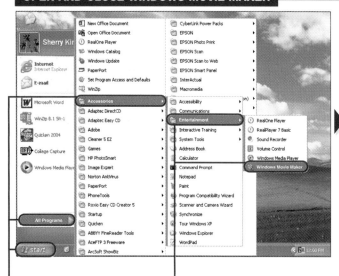

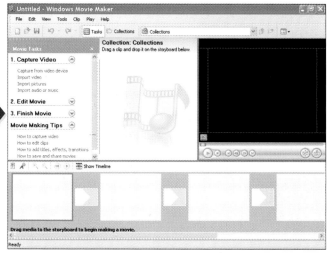

OPEN WINDOWS MOVIE MAKER

1 Click **start**.

2 Click **All Programs**.

3 Click **Accessories**.

4 Click **Entertainment**.

5 Click **Windows Movie Maker**.

■ You can also click **Windows Movie Maker** on the **All Programs** menu.

■ The Windows Movie Maker window appears.

■ You can now capture video footage, import clips, and start creating a video.

Is there a faster way to open Windows Movie Maker?

Yes. If you plan to use the program a lot, you can add a shortcut icon to your Windows XP desktop. See your Windows XP documentation to learn how to add shortcuts to the desktop. While creating the shortcut, you need to locate the executable program file. You can find the Windows Movie Maker program file in the Movie Maker folder within the Program Files folder on your main hard drive.

Should I upgrade to the latest version of Windows Movie Maker?

Yes. The latest version, Windows Movie Maker 2, offers an improved interface, timeline, and more effects, credits, and titles than the previous version. To download the latest version, click **Help** and then click **Windows Movie Maker on the Web**. Log onto your Internet connection and follow the links on the Microsoft Web page to download and install the file.

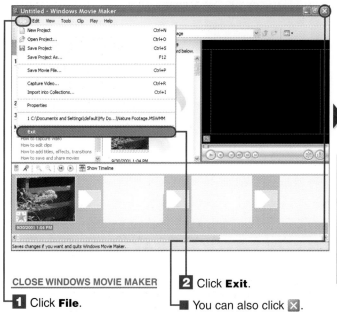

CLOSE WINDOWS MOVIE MAKER

1 Click **File**.

2 Click **Exit**.

■ You can also click ⊠.

■ If you have not saved your work, then click **Yes** in the dialog box that appears.

■ The Windows Movie Maker window closes.

NAVIGATE THE WINDOWS MOVIE MAKER WINDOW

The Windows Movie Maker program window displays several different work areas. If you are new to using Windows Movie Maker, take a moment to familiarize yourself with the program's onscreen elements.

Menu Bar
Displays Windows Movie Maker menus that reveal commands when the user clicks them.

Toolbar
Displays shortcut buttons to Movie Maker commands.

Title Bar
Displays the program name and the name of the open file.

Movie Tasks Pane
Displays shortcut links to common tasks.

Collections Pane
Displays the individual elements that you can include in a movie, such as video clips and photographs.

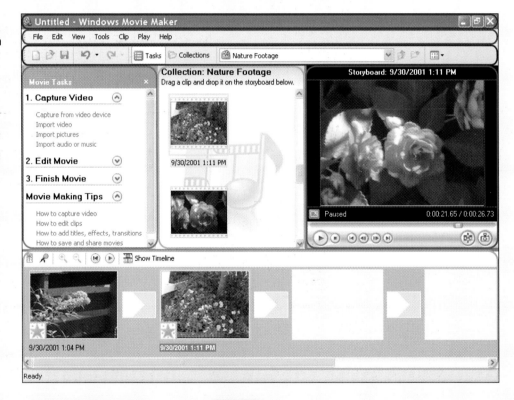

Storyboard/Timeline
Assembles all the video clips and other elements that make up a movie.

Monitor
Lets you preview video clips and the movie.

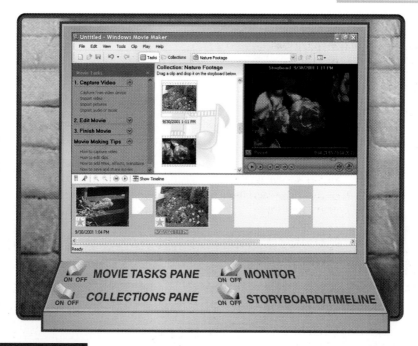

You can hide or display the various window elements in Windows Movie Maker. For example, you may want to close the Movie Tasks pane to see more of your Collections. You can use the View menu to control which program elements display.

ON OFF — MOVIE TASKS PANE
ON OFF — MONITOR
ON OFF — COLLECTIONS PANE
ON OFF — STORYBOARD/TIMELINE

CUSTOMIZE THE PROGRAM ELEMENTS

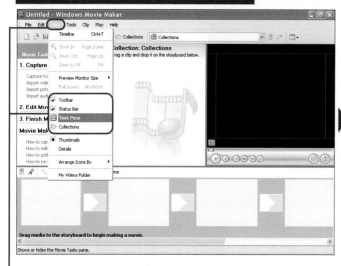

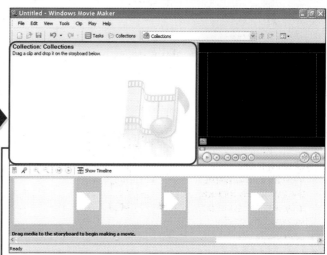

1 Click **View**.

2 Click the program element you want to hide.

■ A check mark or icon appears beside the menu item's name to indicate the item is displaying onscreen.

■ The element that you selected—in this example, the Movie Tasks panel—disappears.

■ You can repeat steps **1** and **2** to display the element again.

RECORD VIDEO FROM A CAMCORDER

You can record video footage directly from your camcorder and import it into Windows Movie Maker. You can accomplish this task, called *capturing*, with the Video Capture Wizard. The Wizard guides you through the necessary steps to prepare the footage for transfer.

To capture footage directly from a camcorder, you must first connect the device to your computer. Depending on the type of device, the connection may require an IEEE 1394, or FireWire, port or card, or a video capture card that you install on your computer. Once you connect the device, turn on the VCR or VTR mode on the camcorder.

RECORD VIDEO FROM A CAMCORDER

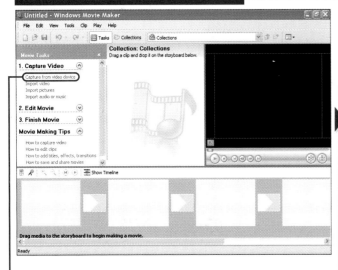

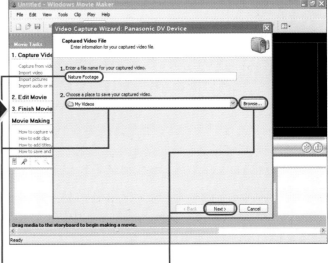

1 Click the **Capture from video device** link.

■ You can also click **File** and then click **Capture Video**.

■ The Video Capture Wizard appears.

Note: If you turn on the video recording device after opening Windows Movie Maker, the Video Capture Wizard may launch automatically.

2 Type a filename for the video footage you want to import into Windows Movie Maker.

3 Click ▼ and specify a folder in which to store the footage.

■ To select another folder for storage, click **Browse**.

4 Click **Next**.

How do I capture video from an analog camcorder or VCR?

Older analog camcorders require a special video capture device, called an *analog-to-digital converter,* to transfer files from the device to your computer. Consult your camcorder manufacturer or a computer store for more information about installing a card in your computer that can communicate with your analog source.

Which video setting is best for capturing footage?

The video setting you select in step **5** below is determined by how you want to use the footage. If you plan to store the movie that you create on your computer for playback, select the **Best quality for playback on my computer** option. If you plan to transfer the finished movie back onto DV tape again, select **Digital device format**. If you plan to use your video footage in other ways, such as for Internet broadcast, select the **Other settings** option and select from the available settings that appear.

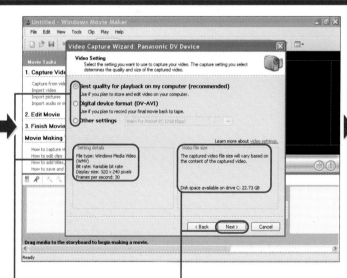

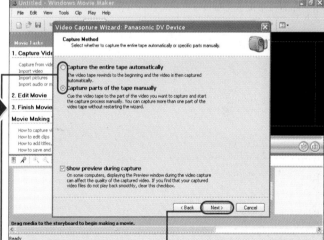

5 Click a video setting (○ changes to ◉).

■ The Setting details area displays information about the file type and movie speed associated with the video setting you select.

■ The Video file size area displays the estimated file size and disk space available.

6 Click **Next**.

7 Click a capture method (○ changes to ◉).

■ Click the first option if you want to capture all of the footage from the tape.

■ Click the second option if you want to manually select which segments of the video you capture from the tape.

8 Click **Next**.

CONTINUED ▶

RECORD VIDEO FROM A CAMCORDER

The Video Capture Wizard lets you control exactly which segments of your video footage you capture for a Windows Movie Maker project. You can select which parts of your video footage you want to turn into a movie. The Video Capture Wizard keeps track of the amount and size of the video footage you capture.

You can view your footage in the Preview area of the Video Capture Wizard dialog box. The Tape position setting beneath the Preview area tracks your exact position in the tape.

RECORD VIDEO FROM A CAMCORDER (CONTINUED)

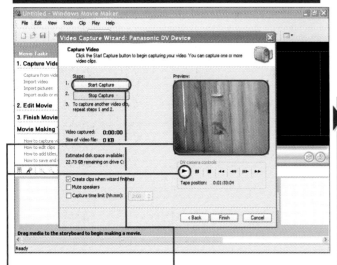

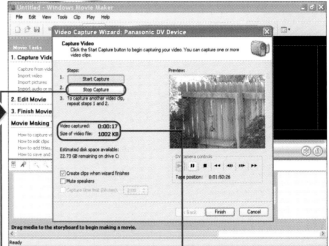

■9 Click the **Play** button (▶).

■ The video footage plays in the Preview area.

■ You can use the DV camera controls to control the camcorder.

Note: If your Video Capture Wizard does not show camera controls, you must manually activate the controls on the camcorder.

■10 When you see a segment that you want to capture, click **Start Capture**.

■ The Video Capture Wizard begins to capture the footage.

■11 When you reach the end of the segment you want, click **Stop Capture**.

■ The Video Capture Wizard displays the video length and size here.

■12 Repeat steps **9** to **11** to continue capturing more video segments.

Where does Windows Movie Maker store my clips if I have not yet saved the project file?

After you capture the clips, the collections file stores your captured clips much like a database file. Although the collections file does not actually contain the clips, it acts as a pointer to the clips. When you save the project, the project file holds all the clips as well as the information about your edits.

CLIPS
• Deer in the Wood
• Mountains
• Duck in Pond
• Landscape

Projects   Collections

Windows Movie Maker created clips for me. How did it know where to divide my video footage?

Windows Movie Maker automatically breaks your video footage into clips based on natural breaks that occurred during shooting. For example, if you turned the camcorder off and on again while shooting, Windows Movie Maker treats the pause as a break when you download the footage into a collection.

Breaking your video footage into clips allows you to work with smaller, more manageable segments when you assemble your final movie.

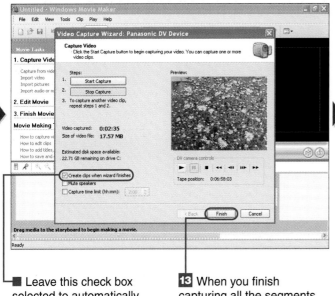

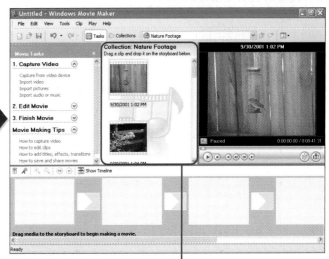

■ Leave this check box selected to automatically import your clips into Windows Movie Maker.

13 When you finish capturing all the segments you want to include in your movie, click **Finish**.

■ Windows Movie Maker closes the Video Capture Wizard and imports the clips.

■ Windows Movie Maker displays the captured clips in the Collections pane.

IMPORT A VIDEO FILE

You can import video files from other sources to your Windows Movie Maker project. For example, you can import a video clip from a friend, or a clip you found on the Internet. When you import a video file, it is stored in a separate collections folder. You can associate it with another collection to keep related items together.

IMPORT A VIDEO FILE

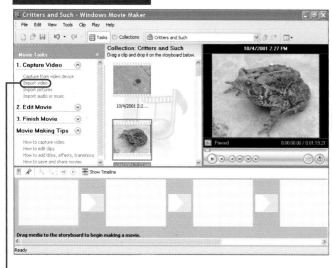

1 Click the **Import video** link.

■ You can also click File and then click **Import into Collections**.

■ The Import File dialog box appears.

2 Navigate to the folder containing the video clip you want to import.

3 Click the video clip.

4 Click **Import**.

How do I import still images?

Windows Movie Maker supports BMP, DIB, EMF, GIF, JPEG, PNG, TIFF, and WMF picture file types. To insert an imported image, drag it from the Collections pane to the frame on the timeline where you want it appear. To import a still image into your movie, follow these steps:

1 Click the **Import pictures** link in the Movie Tasks pane.

■ The Import File dialog box opens.

2 Click the still image file you want to import.

3 Click **Import**.

■ Windows Movie Maker adds the image file to your current collection. You can now drag it to the timeline.

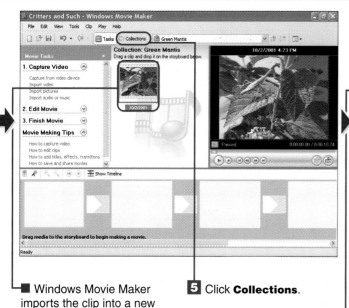

■ Windows Movie Maker imports the clip into a new collection.

5 Click **Collections**.

■ Windows Movie Maker displays the collections hierarchy.

6 Click and drag the clip to the collection to which you want to add the clip.

■ Windows Movie Maker associates the clip with the designated collection.

■ You can click **Tasks** to display the Movie Tasks pane again.

PLAYING

Bike Video

MUSIC OR NARRATION

SOFT   LOUD

SOFT   LOUD

SOUND FROM VIDEO CLIPS

RE

CHAPTER 13

Working with Video Clips in Windows Movie Maker

After you transfer your video footage into Windows Movie Maker, you are ready to begin assembling your project. This chapter shows you how to create and save project files, view and edit clips, and add them to the movie's Storyboard.

PLAY A VIDEO CLIP

You can play clips in the Windows Movie Maker window and preview them in the built-in Monitor, or preview area. Playback controls appear beneath the Monitor for rewinding, fast-forwarding, and moving backward or forward one frame at a time.

PLAY A VIDEO CLIP

■1 In the Collections pane, click the clip you want to view.

■ To view a clip from another collection, click ^ or ˅ to scroll to the other collection.

Note: Collections hold the video footage you capture from your camcorder. See Chapter 12 to learn more about capturing footage and storing clips in collections.

■ Windows Movie Maker displays the clip in the Monitor.

■2 Click the **Play** button (⏵).

Can I view the video clip in full screen mode?

Yes. Click the **View** menu and click **Full Screen**. You can also click the **Full Screen** button (▣) in the Monitor to activate this feature. Windows Movie Maker plays the clip using the full computer monitor screen. When the clip stops playing, click anywhere onscreen to return to the Windows Movie Maker program window.

Can I save a single frame in a clip as an image file?

Yes. Using the playback buttons, navigate to the frame you want to capture and then click the **Take Picture** button (📷). The Save Picture As dialog box appears. Windows Movie Maker can save frames as JPEG files only. Click **Save** to save the image.

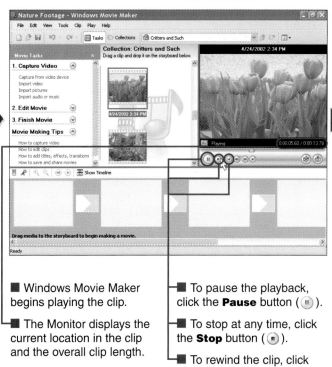

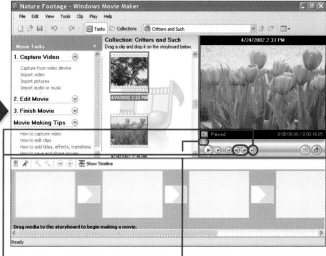

- Windows Movie Maker begins playing the clip.

- The Monitor displays the current location in the clip and the overall clip length.

- To pause the playback, click the **Pause** button (❚❚).

- To stop at any time, click the **Stop** button (■).

- To rewind the clip, click the **Back** button (◀◀).

- To fast-forward the clip, click the **Forward** button (▶).

- To move backward or forward one frame at a time, click the **Previous Frame** (◀) or **Next Frame** (▶) buttons.

- When the clip plays to the end, Windows Movie Maker moves the playback icon to the beginning of the clip.

RENAME A VIDEO CLIP

By default, Windows Movie Maker names your captured video clips based on the date and time they are recorded with the Video Capture Wizard. In the Collections pane, you can give the clips more distinctive names to help you identify them easily.

RENAME A VIDEO CLIP

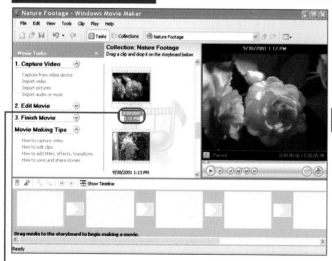

1 In the Collections pane, click the clip name you want to change.

■ Windows Movie Maker highlights the current name.

2 Type a new name for the clip.

3 Press the Enter key.

■ Windows Movie Maker renames the clip.

REMOVE A CLIP FROM A COLLECTION

You can remove a clip you no longer need. For example, you may want to remove a clip that was shot under poor lighting conditions, or one that does not fit into your project theme. When you remove a clip, Windows Movie Maker deletes it from the collection as well as the current project file.

If you delete a clip and find out you need it again later, you must import the clip into your collection again or recapture the video segment from your camcorder again.

REMOVE A CLIP FROM A COLLECTION

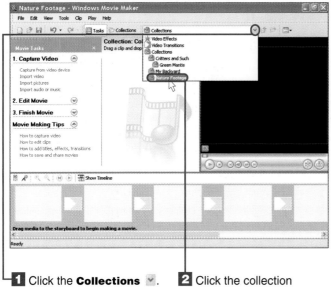

1 Click the **Collections** ☑.

2 Click the collection containing the clip you want to delete.

3 In the Collections pane, click the clip you want to delete.

4 Click **Edit**.

5 Click **Delete**.

■ You can also right-click the clip and then click **Delete**.

■ Windows Movie Maker removes the clip from the collection.

*Note: If you accidentally remove a clip you need, you must immediately click the **Undo** button (☑) to undo the process.*

ADD A CLIP TO THE STORYBOARD

You can use the Storyboard to assemble video clips and build a movie. The Storyboard appears as a linear sequence of boxes, which represent clips, at the bottom of the Windows Movie Maker program window. You can assemble clips in any order you want. The movie plays the clips in sequence, from left to right in the Storyboard.

After you assemble your Storyboard, you can switch to Timeline view to add background music and narration, based on the timing of each clip. See Chapter 14 to learn more about working with the Timeline to add effects and music to your movie.

ADD A CLIP TO THE STORYBOARD

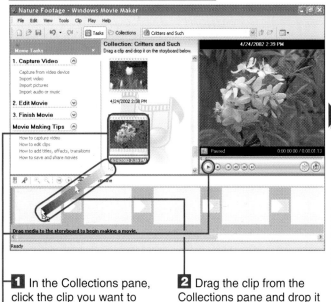

1 In the Collections pane, click the clip you want to add.

■ To view the clip in the Monitor first, click the **Play** button (▶).

2 Drag the clip from the Collections pane and drop it where you want it to appear in the Storyboard.

■ Windows Movie Maker adds the clip to the Storyboard.

You can change the order of clips in your movie by changing their location in the Storyboard. For example, you may want to move a short clip to the beginning to use as a background for a title.

REARRANGE STORYBOARD CLIPS

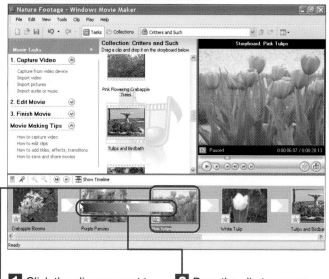

1 Click the clip you want to move.

2 Drag the clip to a new location on the Storyboard.

■ Windows Movie Maker moves the clip.

■ Windows Movie Maker automatically adjusts the remaining Storyboard clips.

REMOVE A CLIP FROM THE STORYBOARD

You can remove a video clip from the Storyboard to delete the clip from your movie. For example, you may want to remove a clip that is too slow or poorly shot.

When you remove a clip from the Storyboard, it remains in the collection in which it is originally associated.

REMOVE A CLIP FROM THE STORYBOARD

1 Right-click the clip you want to remove.

2 Click **Delete**.

Note: See the section "Remove a Clip from a Collection" to learn how to permanently remove a video clip.

■ Windows Movie Maker removes the clip from the Storyboard.

■ Windows Movie Maker automatically adjusts the remaining Storyboard clips.

SAVE A PROJECT FILE

After you capture video
clips to use in a project
and begin assembling
them in the Storyboard,
you can save your work
as a Windows Movie
Maker project file.
Saving a project allows
you to return to the file
later to apply more
edits. Windows Movie
Maker saves project
files in the MSWMM
file format.

A project file includes
the clips you add to the
Timeline and all the edits
you make to the clips. The
project file does not include
the final movie that you
create using the clips.

SAVE A PROJECT FILE

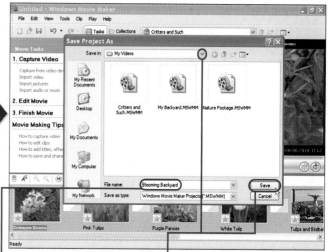

1 Click the **Save Project**
button (⊞).

■ You can also click the **File**
menu and then click **Save**.

■ The Save Project As
dialog box appears.

2 Type a filename for the
project.

■ To save the project in
another folder, click here and
navigate to the folder.

3 Click **Save**.

■ Windows Movie Maker
saves the project file.

CREATE A NEW PROJECT

You can create a new project file any time you want to start a new movie. You can even use the same captured video clips in a new project, but assemble them in a different way, or you can add different transition effects.

CREATE A NEW PROJECT

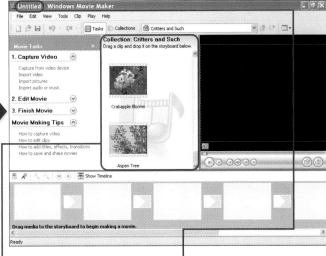

1 Click the **New Project** button (▢).

■ You can also click the **File** menu and then click **New Project**.

■ Windows Movie Maker opens a new project file.

■ Windows Movie Maker displays the collection you were working with in your last session.

■ The project remains untitled until you save the file.

Note: See the previous section to learn how to save a project.

You can open a previously saved project file to continue to work on your movie. You can open only one project file at a time in Windows Movie Maker. Video files consume a lot of processing power, so opening one file at a time allows your computer to run more efficiently.

OPEN AN EXISTING PROJECT

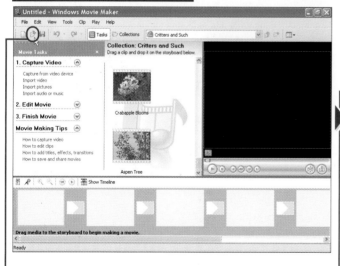

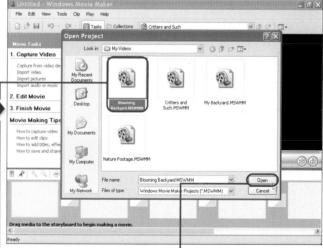

1 Click the **Open Project** button (🖻).

■ You can also click the **File** menu and then click **Open Project**.

■ The Open Project dialog box appears.

2 Click the project you want to open.

3 Click **Open**.

■ Windows Movie Maker opens the file.

TRIM A CLIP

You can edit a video clip by trimming off the beginning or end of the clip. Trimming a clip can help you to reduce the playing time of a video segment, or to cut out extra footage that you do not want to appear in your final movie. Trimming clips can also help reduce your overall file size. Trimming a clip does not alter the original footage.

You can trim clips in Timeline view. Trimming a clip does not affect the original clip that you store in the project file and list in the clip collection. To trim a clip, you adjust the clip's *trim points*, the beginning or end borders of the clip.

TRIM A CLIP

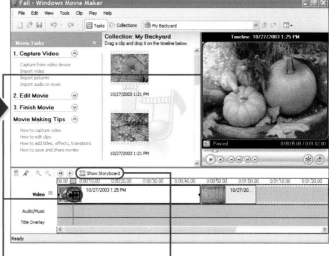

1 Click the **Show Timeline** button (Show Timeline).

■ Windows Movie Maker switches the Storyboard to Timeline view.

2 Drag the clip's trim point to trim the clip.

■ The cursor becomes a red ◄—►.

■ The Monitor plays the clip forward or backward, depending on the direction you drag the clip border.

3 Release the mouse button to trim the clip.

■ You can click the **Show Storyboard** button (Show Storyboard) to return to the Storyboard view.

You can split a longer clip into two clips. For example, you may want to cut a clip in the middle in order to use the first part of the clip in your movie. Splitting a clip allows you to work with both halves separately.

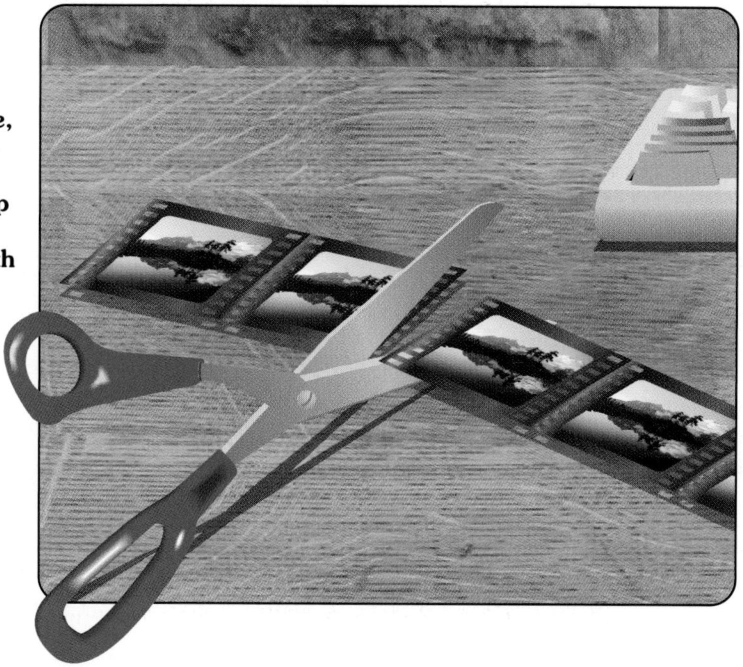

It is a good idea to rename your split clips so that you can keep track of them. See the section "Rename a Video Clip" earlier in this chapter for more information.

SPLIT A CLIP

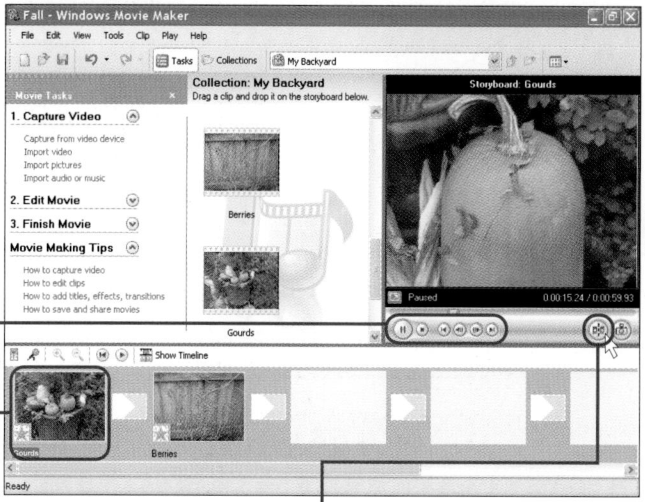

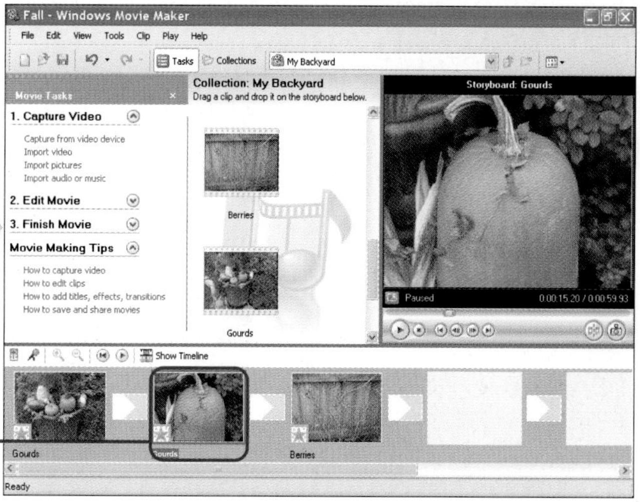

1 Click the clip you want to split in the Storyboard.

2 Using the playback controls, navigate to the frame at which you want to split the clip.

■ You can use the **Pause** button ( ) to pause at the frame where you want to split the clip.

3 Click the **Split** button ( ).

■ Windows Movie Maker splits the original clip and creates a new clip from the second half of the original clip.

■ You can rename the second clip to distinguish it from the original clip.

Note: See the next section to learn how to recombine clips.

COMBINE TWO CLIPS

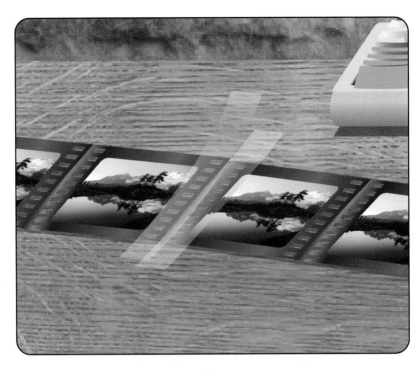

You can combine two or more contiguous clips in your Storyboard to create one large clip. When you combine multiple clips, Windows Movie Maker assigns the first clip's name to the resulting clip. You can only combine clips that have been split previously.

COMBINE TWO CLIPS

1 Click the first clip you want to combine in the Storyboard.

2 Press and hold **Ctrl** while clicking the other clip you want to combine.

3 Click **Clip**.

4 Click **Combine**.

Note: See the previous section to learn how to split a clip.

■ Windows Movie Maker combines the clips you selected into one clip.

PREVIEW A MOVIE

After adding video clips to the Storyboard, you can preview the movie to see how the clips play sequentially. Your movie plays in the same Monitor as individual video clips.

PREVIEW A MOVIE

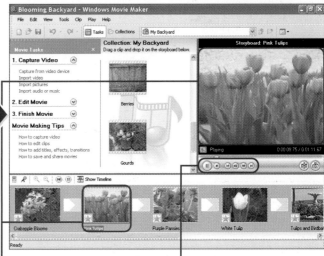

1 Click the first clip in the Storyboard.

2 Click the **Play** button (▶).

Note: You can switch to Timeline view and watch the Playhead move from frame to frame as the movie plays each clip.

■ Windows Movie Maker plays the movie.

■ A highlight border appears around the currently playing clip in the Storyboard area.

■ You can use the playback buttons to stop or pause the movie.

Note: See the section "Play a Video Clip" at the beginning of this chapter to learn more about using the playback controls.

CHAPTER 14

Adding Extra Effects to Video Clips in Windows Movie Maker

After you assemble the clips that make up your movie, you can add extra effects to your project, such as transitions, special effects, and text elements. This chapter shows you how to add title text and credits, transitions between scenes, music, and narration.

USING THE TIMELINE

You can toggle to Timeline view to see your movie's *tracks* — the linear representations of clips and other media that you add to the movie. You can assemble and edit clips in Timeline view just as you do in Storyboard view. For example, you can trim the length of a clip in Timeline view, or see how an overlay of title text appears with other clips in the movie.

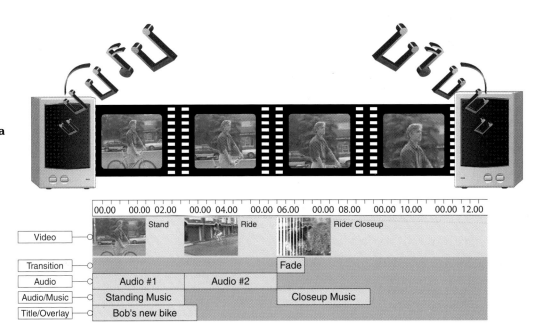

USING THE TIMELINE

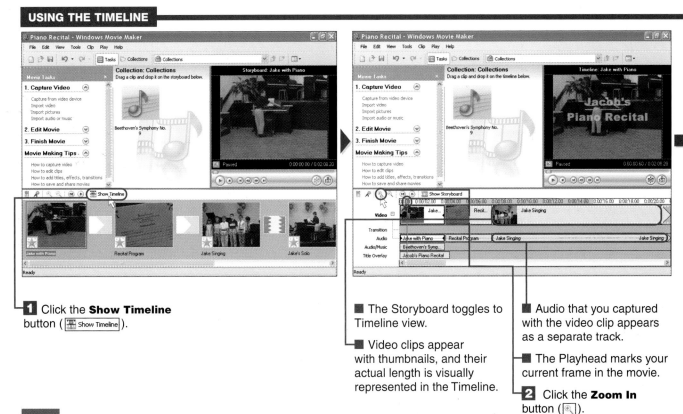

1 Click the **Show Timeline** button (⊞ Show Timeline).

■ The Storyboard toggles to Timeline view.

■ Video clips appear with thumbnails, and their actual length is visually represented in the Timeline.

■ Audio that you captured with the video clip appears as a separate track.

■ The Playhead marks your current frame in the movie.

2 Click the **Zoom In** button (🔍).

236

Can I make my Timeline larger?

Yes. To enlarge the Timeline/Storyboard area, move the mouse pointer over the top border of the Timeline until it becomes a double-sided arrow pointer. Click and drag the border to adjust the Timeline size.

How do I play a movie from the Timeline?

Drag the Playhead to the frame from which you want to start the playback and then click the **Play Timeline** button (⊡). You can also click the **Play** button (⊡) on the Monitor's playback controls. To quickly move the Playhead back to the beginning of the movie, click the **Rewind Timeline** button (⊡).

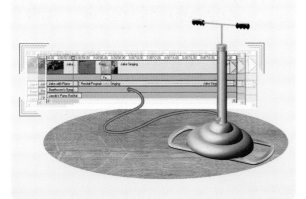

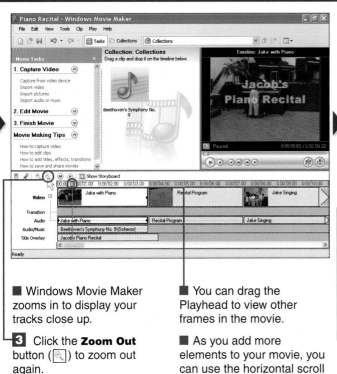

■ Windows Movie Maker zooms in to display your tracks close up.

3 Click the **Zoom Out** button (⊡) to zoom out again.

■ You can drag the Playhead to view other frames in the movie.

■ As you add more elements to your movie, you can use the horizontal scroll bar to view different tracks along the Timeline.

■ Transition effects that you add to clips appear in the Transition track.

■ Title or credit text that you overlay on other clips appears in the Title Overlay track.

■ Additional audio clips that you add appear in the Audio/Music track.

ADD TITLE AND CREDIT TEXT

You can add titles and credits to your movie, and specify how you want them to appear. You can make your text appear at the beginning or end of a movie, or as an overlay that displays over the video clips. Windows Movie Maker treats your text as a separate video clip in your movie.

Title text usually appears at the beginning of a movie, while credits appear at the end. You can choose to add your title and credit text where they work best.

ADD TITLE AND CREDIT TEXT

1 Click the **Show Timeline** button ![Show Timeline].

■ The Storyboard toggles to Timeline view.

2 Click **Tools**.

3 Click **Titles and Credits**.

How do I fix a mistake in the title text?

You can return to the Movie Tasks pane and edit your title text. Simply right-click the text clip in the Timeline or Storyboard, and then click **Edit Title**. The text-editing window appears, allowing you to make your corrections. To apply your changes to the text clip, click **Done, add title to movie**.

Why does the Enter Text for Title page display two text boxes?

You can enter title text in the top box. If your title requires a second line of text, you can type the additional text in the second box. This allows you to format the two text box items independently. For example, you can make the first line of text large and bold, and the second line smaller and not bold.

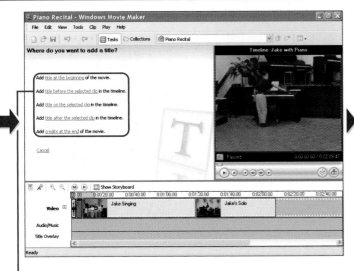

■ Text and credit options appear in the Movie Tasks pane.

4 Click an option to specify how you want to display the text in your movie.

■ You can choose to display text as a separate title clip or as an overlay track that plays on top of your existing clips.

■ A template appears, depending on the option you selected.

5 Type the text you want to add as your title or credits.

■ The Monitor displays how your text will appear.

CONTINUED

ADD TITLE AND CREDIT TEXT

After you type your text, you can use the remaining pages in the Movie Tasks pane to add animation effects and change the text formatting. Animation effects control how the text appears, for example, fading in or out. Text formatting controls include options for specifying a font, increasing or decreasing the font size, changing the font color, and even setting an alignment position for the text.

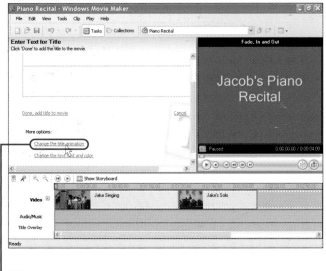

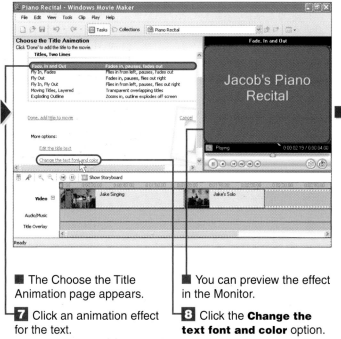

6 Click the **Change the title animation** option.

■ You may need to scroll down the Movie Tasks pane to view the option.

■ The Choose the Title Animation page appears.

7 Click an animation effect for the text.

■ You can preview the effect in the Monitor.

8 Click the **Change the text font and color** option.

How do I remove title text I no longer need?

To remove a text clip from your Storyboard, click the text clip, and then press the ☒ key. Windows Movie Maker permanently removes the text clip from your movie. To add the clip back again, you must repeat the steps for adding text or credits.

Can I control the duration of my title or credit text?

Yes. Switch to Timeline view, click the clip you want to change, and then drag a trim point to increase or decrease the text clip's duration. If your text clip appears as an overlay, select the clip in the Title Overlay track and then drag a trim point to adjust the clip's duration.

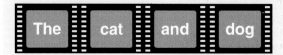

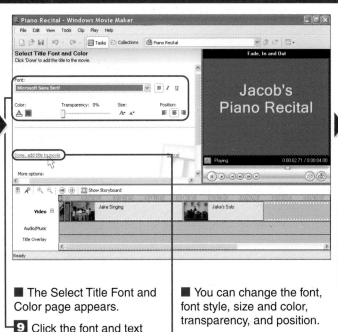

■ The Select Title Font and Color page appears.

9 Click the font and text color options you want to assign.

■ You can change the font, font style, size and color, transparency, and position.

10 Click **Done, add title to movie**.

■ Windows Movie Maker adds the text to your movie as a video clip.

■ If you applied the overlay option to the title, then the text clip would appear in the Title Overlay track of the Timeline.

ADD A TRANSITION EFFECT

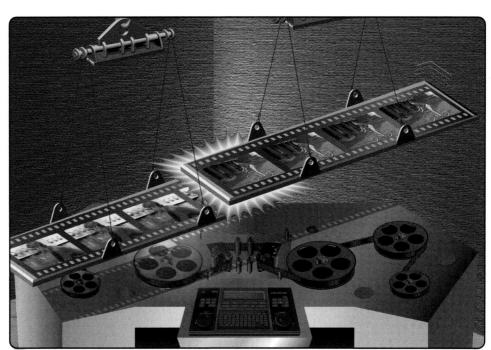

You can add transition effects to your movie to control how one clip changes to another clip. Without a transition effect between clips, the movie abruptly plays one clip right after the next clip ends. Windows Movie Maker includes a variety of transitions, ranging from a simple fade in/fade out, to more complex transition effects, such as rotation and film-aging effects.

ADD A TRANSITION EFFECT

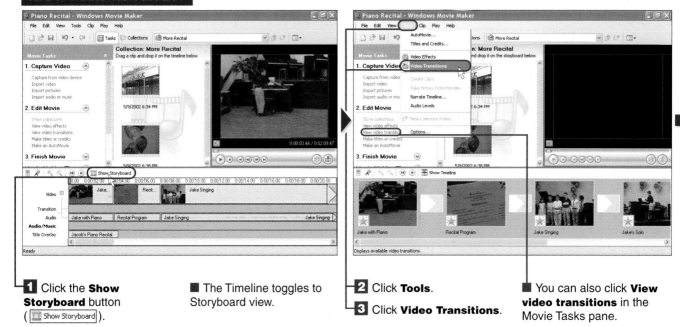

1 Click the **Show Storyboard** button (Show Storyboard).

■ The Timeline toggles to Storyboard view.

2 Click **Tools**.

3 Click **Video Transitions**.

■ You can also click **View video transitions** in the Movie Tasks pane.

How do I add a transition in Timeline view?

Select the clip that you want to precede with a transition. Open the Video Transitions pane and select the transition you want to add. Click the **Clip** menu and then click **Add to Timeline**. Windows Movie Maker applies the transition and displays a bar in the Transition track of the Timeline.

Can I replace an existing transition with a new transition?

Yes. The easiest way to swap transition effects is to drag a new transition to the transition area between two clips in Storyboard view. If you prefer to delete a transition entirely, click the transition area between two clips and press the ⊠ key.

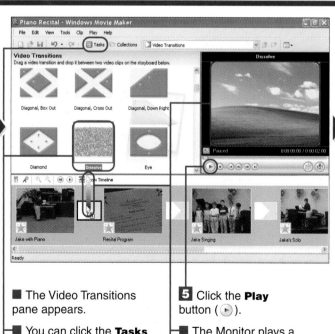

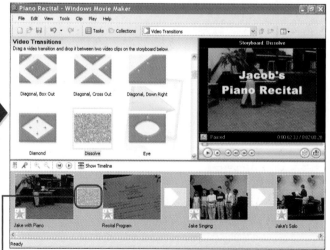

■ The Video Transitions pane appears.

■ You can click the **Tasks** button (☐ Tasks) to hide the Movie Tasks pane and view more effects.

4 Click an effect.

5 Click the **Play** button (▶).

■ The Monitor plays a sample of the transition.

6 Drag a transition from the pane and drop it on the Storyboard where you want it to occur.

■ Windows Movie Maker assigns the transition between the two clips.

■ You can continue adding more effects to your movie.

Note: To replace the Video Transitions page with another page, click the Collections ⌄ and select another collection.

ADD A VIDEO EFFECT

You can add special effects to your movie in Windows Movie Maker to make your movie more interesting. These video effects range from fading and blurring to an artistic watercolor or aged-film appearance. You can apply an effect to an individual clip or to all of the clips in your movie.

You can add video effects in Storyboard or Timeline view. When you add an effect, it appears as a star icon on the clip in either view.

ADD A VIDEO EFFECT

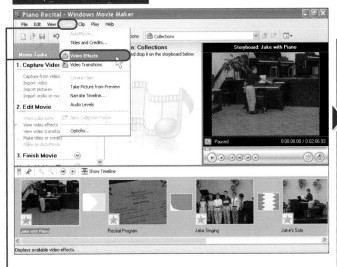

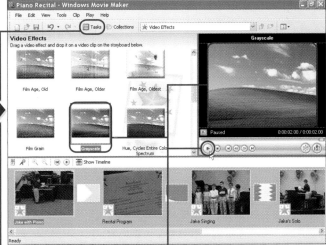

1 Click **Tools**.

2 Click **Video Effects**.

■ You can also click **View video effects** in the Movie Tasks pane.

*Note: To apply an effect to all of the clips in your movie, click the **Edit** menu and then click **Select All** or press* Ctrl + A *before applying the effect.*

■ The Video Effects page appears.

■ You can click the **Tasks** button (Tasks) to hide the Movie Tasks pane and view more effects.

3 Click an effect.

4 Click the **Play** button (▶).

■ The Monitor plays a sample of the effect.

Can I add more than one effect to a single clip?

Yes. For example, to give a clip an aged appearance, you can combine two aging effects to create the look you want, such as Grayscale and Film Age Older. You can add multiple effects using the steps in this section, or you can apply them all at once using the Add or Remove Video Effects dialog box. Right-click the clip and select **Video Effects** to open the dialog box. Click the Add and Remove buttons to add more effects or remove effects you do not want. Keep in mind that, unlike the Video Effects pane, you cannot preview the effects in this dialog box.

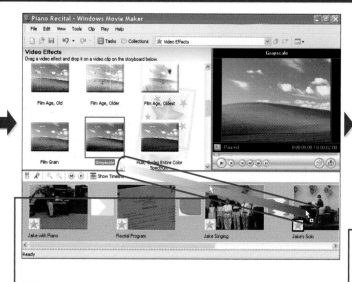

5 To apply an effect, drag it onto the clip.

■ Windows Movie Maker assigns the effect and highlights the effect icon on the clip in Storyboard view.

IMPORT AN AUDIO CLIP

You can import audio clips to play in your movie. For example, you can add a music clip to play in the background, or add some sound-effect clips to play at certain points in the movie for added drama.

When you import an audio clip, Windows Movie Maker stores the clip in a collection. You can access the collection at any time to use the clip in as many movies as you like. Windows Movie Maker supports a variety of audio file formats, including WAV, AIF, AU, and MP3.

IMPORT AN AUDIO CLIP

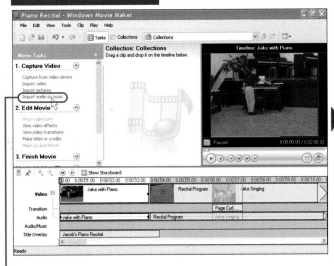

1 In the Movie Tasks pane, click **Import audio or music**.

■ You can also click the **File** menu and then click **Import into Collections**.

■ The Import File dialog box appears.

2 Click the clip you want to import.

3 Click **Import**.

■ Windows Movie Maker imports the clip into a new collection.

ADD AN AUDIO CLIP

Although most video captures include audio along with the video footage, you can also add other audio clips to play in your movie. For example, you can add background music or sound effects. Additional audio clips appear in the Audio/Music track in the movie's Timeline.

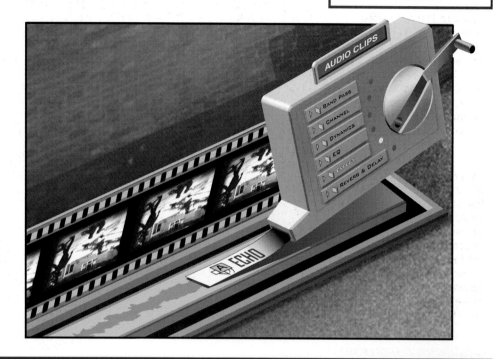

ADD AN AUDIO CLIP

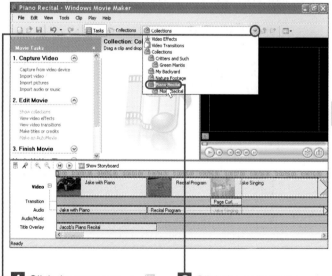

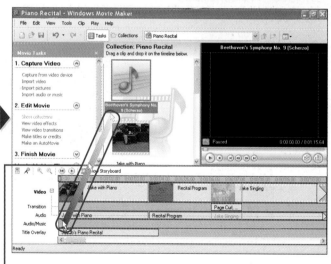

1 Click the **Collections** ⌄.

2 Click the collection containing the audio clip you want to add.

■ The collection page appears for the collection you selected.

3 Drag the clip to the Timeline and drop it on the Audio/Music track where you want it to play.

■ Windows Movie Maker adds the clip to the movie.

ADJUST AUDIO LEVELS

When you add new audio clips to your movie, they play simultaneously with existing audio that you recorded with the video footage. To control how the audio tracks play, you can open the Audio Levels dialog box and adjust the mix between recorded audio and additional audio tracks.

ADJUST AUDIO LEVELS

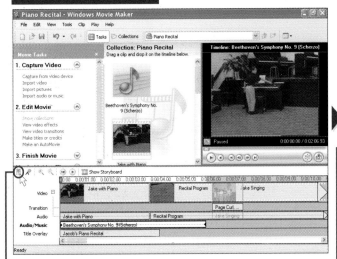

1 Click the **Set Audio Levels** button (⊞) in Timeline view.

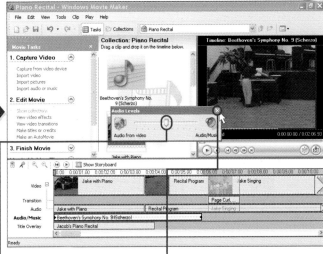

■ The Audio Levels dialog box appears.

2 Drag ▯ to adjust the audio mix.

■ Drag ▯ to the left to increase the video track's audio.

■ Drag ▯ to the right to increase the audio or music clip level.

■ If you drag ▯ all the way to either end, this mutes the other track.

3 Click ✕ to exit the dialog box.

EDIT AUDIO CLIPS

You can edit individual audio clips that you add to your movie. For example, you may want to mute a clip while you play the movie in the Timeline, or fade a music clip in or out. You can also set a volume level for a clip to control how it plays in the movie.

EDIT AUDIO CLIPS

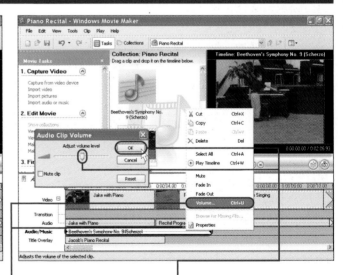

CHANGE AUDIO SETTINGS

1 Right-click the audio clip you want to edit.

2 Select the audio setting you want to apply.

■ Windows Movie Maker applies the new setting to the clip.

ADJUST VOLUME LEVELS

1 Right-click the audio clip you want to edit.

2 Click **Volume**.

■ The Audio Clip Volume dialog box appears.

3 Drag ▯ to adjust the volume level.

4 Click **OK**.

■ Windows Movie Maker applies the new setting to the clip.

RECORD NARRATION

You can record a narration track to accompany your movie clips. For example, you can record a narration that explains your family vacation video. To record your own narration, you need to connect a microphone to your computer.

Jim is demonstrating the experimental XP51 bicycle. It has been streamlined and features better braking with a more comfortable riding position.

After you record the narration, Windows Movie Maker treats it like any other audio clip in your Timeline. The narration clip is also added to a collection. You can find your Audio/Music clip in the Audio/Music track on the movie's Timeline.

RECORD NARRATION

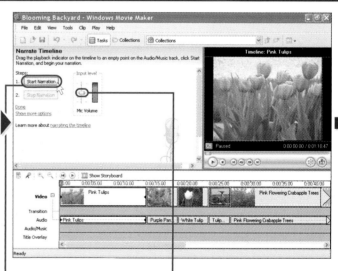

1 Move the Playhead in Timeline view to the frame where you want to start recording.

2 Click the **Narrate Timeline** button (🖉).

■ You can also click the **Tools** menu and then click **Narrate Timeline**.

■ The Narrate Timeline page appears.

3 Click the **Start Narration** button and begin talking into the microphone.

■ Windows Movie Maker begins playing your movie so that you can synchronize the narration with the video footage.

■ You can drag the Input Level ⬜ to increase or decrease the volume of your narration.

My narration competes with the audio that I recorded with the video footage. How do I turn off the audio from the video footage?

You can mute the audio from the video footage. To do this, right-click the track in the Timeline that you want to control, and then click **Mute** in the pop-up menu that appears.

How do I remove a narration clip from my movie?

To remove a narration clip, select the clip in the Timeline, and then click the ⊠ button. Windows Movie Maker removes the clip from the Timeline, although the recorded narration file remains in the collection where you saved it.

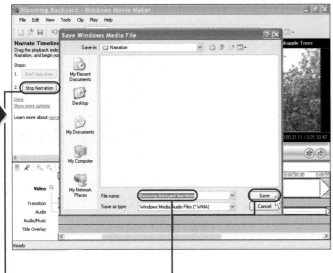

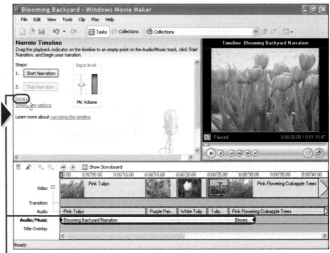

4 When you finish with your narration, click **Stop Narration**.

■ The Save Windows Media File dialog box appears.

5 Type a filename for the narration file or use the default name.

6 Click **Save**.

■ The narration now appears as a track in your movie's Timeline.

7 Click **Done**.

■ Windows Movie Maker closes the Narrate Timeline page.

SAVE A MOVIE

After you add the transitions, video effects, and audio clips to your movie, you can save your final product as a movie file to share with others. You can use the Save Movie Wizard to specify where to save the movie file, create a name for the file, and specify any quality settings.

Once you save a movie file, you cannot edit the movie file again. Windows Movie Maker saves movie files in the Windows Media (WMV) format. You cannot view movie files in Windows Movie Maker.

SAVE A MOVIE

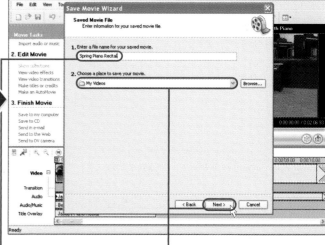

1 Click **Save to my computer**.

■ To save the movie to another location, such as a CD-ROM or e-mail message, select the location option for your movie file.

■ You can also click the **File** menu and then click **Save Movie File**.

■ The Save Movie Wizard appears.

2 Type a filename for the movie.

3 Click the ⌄ and select a destination for the file, or leave the default folder selected.

4 Click **Next**.

**How is saving a movie different from
saving a project?**

When you save a movie, you create a
new and complete file that turns all the
individual clips, transitions, and
other effects into a single
movie. When you save a
project, you save the
individual elements of
the movie, as well as
your current edits. A
project file is an
editable file, while
a movie file cannot
be edited.

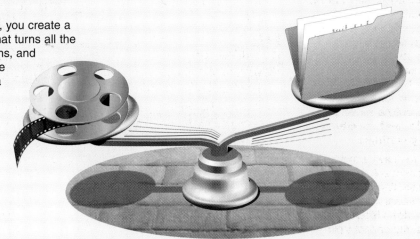

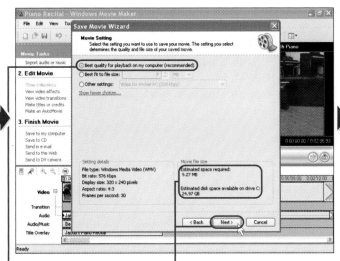

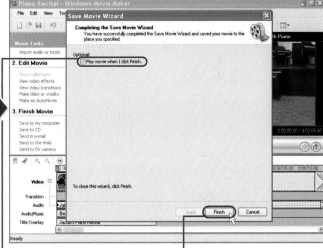

■ The Movie Setting page
appears.

5 Click a movie setting or
leave the default setting
selected (○ changes to ◉).

■ To see additional options,
click **Show more choices**,
or to hide the additional
settings, click **Show fewer
choices**.

■ Details about the file size
appear here.

6 Click **Next**.

■ The wizard advances to
the last page.

■ You can leave this option
selected to view your movie
in Windows Media Player
after saving the file.

7 Click **Finish**.

■ Windows Movie Maker
may take several minutes to
save the movie, depending
on the movie size.

CHAPTER 15

Downloading and Recording Video Files

This chapter shows you how to download video clips from the Internet and store them on your computer, burn video CDs or DVDs, and share your video files with other users.

DOWNLOAD AND SAVE A VIDEO CLIP

You can download video clips from the Internet and store them on your hard drive. For example, if friends or family members post a home-video clip of their baby's first steps on their Web site, you can download and save the clip on your computer. You can then use Windows Media Player to view the clip. Windows Media Player supports MPEG, AVI, and SWF file types.

You cannot save copyrighted video clips on your computer. Many companies that offer streaming audio and video clips on the Web support view-only clips to comply with copyright laws. This means that you can view the clips but not save them to your computer.

DOWNLOAD AND SAVE A VIDEO CLIP

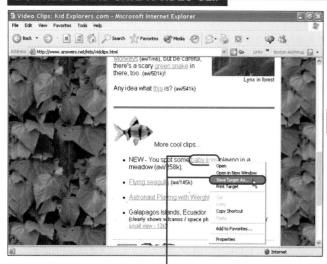

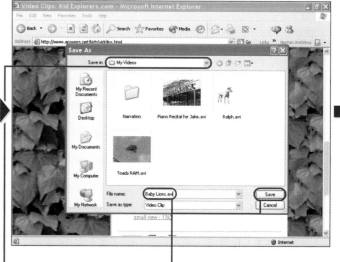

1 Open your Web browser window to the Web page containing the clip that you want to download.

2 Right-click over the video link.

3 Click **Save Target As**.

■ The Save As dialog box appears.

4 Specify a destination folder for the clip.

■ You can type a new filename here.

5 Click **Save**.

■ The clip starts downloading.

How do I view a clip on the Web without saving the file?

You can simply click a video clip link and view the video clip immediately without saving it to your computer. This is only possible with file types registered to play in Internet Explorer. Depending on the size of the clip, the video may take a few moments to download before playback starts.

How do I find free clips to view?

You can conduct a Web search for free video clips. There are plenty of sites that offer free clips that you can download, save, and share with others. For example, WMV clips, a common Windows video format, are easy to download and take up little space on your computer.

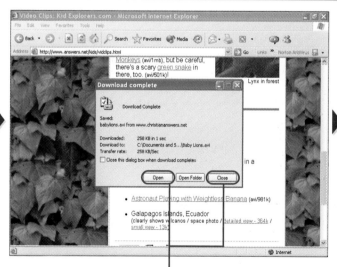

■ When the clip finishes downloading, the Download complete dialog box appears.

6 Click **Open** to view the clip now.

■ You can click **Close** if you want to view the clip later.

■ Windows Media Player opens and plays the clip.

BURN VIDEO FILES TO A CD OR DVD

You can copy, or *burn*, video files from your computer onto a CD or DVD. Burning your own CDs and DVDs is a great way to share your video creations and home movies with others. In order to burn your own videos, you need a CD or DVD burner and software.

Windows XP does not offer built-in support for DVD burning. You can use the software that came with your CD or DVD burner to copy files to a CD or DVD.

BURN VIDEO FILES TO A CD OR DVD

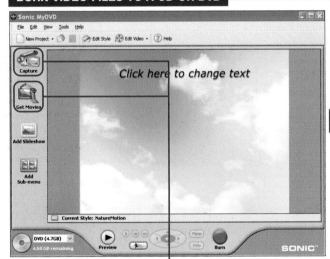

1 Insert a blank CD or DVD into your computer's CD or DVD drive.

2 Launch the software that came with the drive for creating CDs or DVDs.

■ This example uses Sonic MyDVD to burn a DVD.

■ You can add video directly from a camcorder device.

■ You can add clips from your hard drive.

3 Click the **Get Movies** option.

Note: Your software may utilize a different command or menu step to add movie clips.

■ The Add movie(s) to menu dialog box appears.

4 Click the video file you want to add.

■ To add multiple files, press and hold the **Shift** or **Ctrl** key while clicking filenames.

5 Click **Open**.

258

What are some other good video-burning applications I can use?

Nero 6 (www.nero.com), Roxio Easy CD and DVD Creator (www.roxio.com), and WinDVD Creator Plus (www.intervideo.com) are just a few of the popular CD- and DVD-burning programs that are available today. You can also find free programs on the Internet. DVD Wizard Pro and DVD X Copy Xpress are two examples. You can also find DVD burners that offer trial versions. These let you try the product for a set amount of time or usage before making a purchase decision.

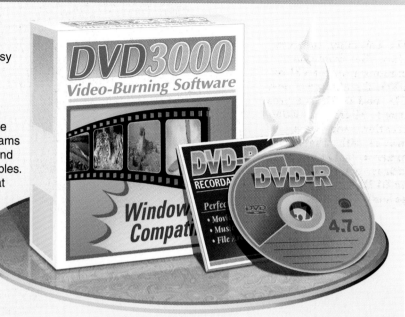

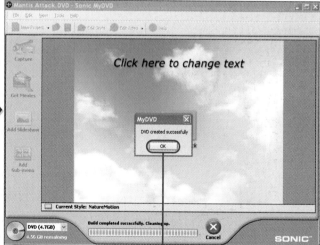

6 Click **Burn**.

■ The program begins burning the video file or files to the CD or DVD.

Note: Burning video CDs or DVDs can take a long time, depending on the file size. For example, a 60-minute video may take 4 hours to encode and another 30 minutes to burn onto a CD or DVD.

■ A dialog box appears when the burning process is complete.

7 Click **OK**.

■ You can now view the video on the CD or DVD.

SHARE VIDEOS ON YOUR COMPUTER

You can share your video files with others who use your computer. Ordinarily, videos that you save in the My Videos folder, or any other folder in the My Documents folder, are only accessible by you. When you copy a video file to the Shared Documents folder, the video is available to other users who log into the computer with a different login.

SHARE VIDEOS ON YOUR COMPUTER

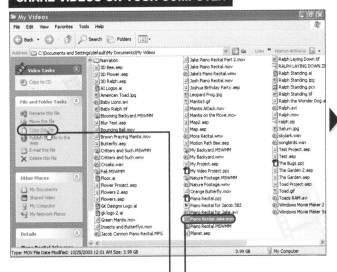

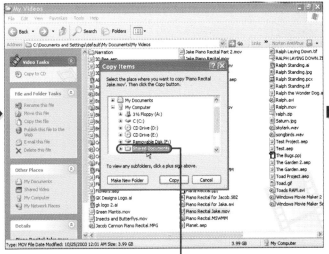

COPY THE VIDEO FILE

1 Open the folder containing the video file you want to share.

2 Click the filename.

3 Click the **Copy this file** link.

■ The Copy Items dialog box appears.

4 Click the **Shared Documents** folder to expand its contents.

Is there any way to speed up the video-copying process?

Not really. You can reduce the video file size by saving it to another file format, or by making adjustments to the video quality. The higher the quality, the larger the file size becomes. If the program you use to create a video file allows you to set quality levels, consider setting levels for Internet-based transmission, which makes the video content easy to transfer and view over the Internet.

Can I lock my video files to prevent unauthorized use?

The best way to guard your files is to create a login password so others cannot log into your computer and view your files. See your Windows XP documentation to learn how to set up and store a password. If you share your computer with other users, make sure each user has his or her own login and password.

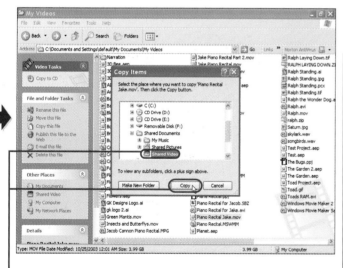

5 Click the **Shared Video** folder.

6 Click **Copy**.

■ Windows XP begins copying the file.

■ Depending on the file size, the process may take several minutes or hours.

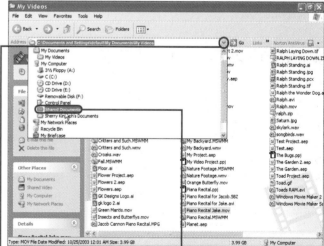

VIEW THE SHARED DOCUMENTS FOLDER

1 Click ⌄ to view the Shared Documents folder and subfolders.

2 Click **Shared Documents**.

■ Windows XP opens the Shared Documents folder view, allowing you to open the Shared Video folder and see the copied file.

CHAPTER 16

Playing Windows XP Games

The term multimedia *really comes to life in computer games. Games combine audio, video, images, and animations to create interactive worlds and game play. This chapter shows you how to get started using Windows XP games.*

INTRODUCTION TO WINDOWS XP GAMES

You can play games for entertainment on your computer. Windows XP comes with several singleplayer and multiplayer games. If you are new to the Windows XP games, it is a good idea to become familiar with what games are available.

The multiplayer Internet games, which include Backgammon, Checkers, Hearts, Reversi, and Spades, allow you to play with other users online. See the section "Play a Multiplayer Game" later in this chapter to learn more about online games.

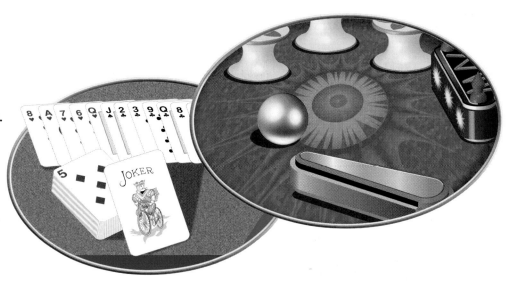

FreeCell

A variation of the solitaire card game, FreeCell is one of the more challenging games offered by Windows XP. It requires you to build descending columns of cards on opposite colors and then to transfer the cards in ascending order to one of four free cells at the top right area of the window. In addition, you can use four other free cells to help you move cards from one stack and wait for another spot to open up. A free cell can only hold one card at a time.

Hearts

Hearts is a classic four-person card game, and in the Windows XP version, you can play against three computer players. The object of the game is to finish with the lowest score. You accumulate points at the end of each hand based on how many hearts you are holding, and an automatic 13 points if you have the queen of spades. The game continues until one of the players accumulates 100 points.

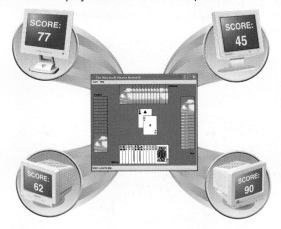

Minesweeper

Minesweeper is a logic game in which you try to determine the location of various hidden mines on the grid. If you click a square containing a mine, then it blows up and you lose. A timer keeps track of the playing time, and a scoreboard keeps track of your score.

Pinball

Pinball is a virtual arcade game based on the classic pinball machine. The object is to make the pinball stay in play for as long as possible, accumulating points along the way. You can use the keyboard's spacebar to launch the pinball, and the Z and / keys to move the left and right flippers.

Solitaire

Solitaire is an addictive game based on the traditional card game. The object of the game is to build up four suit stacks, in ascending order, starting with the aces. You can place cards on alternate colors to keep your playing stacks and draw pile changing. You can use the Options feature to change how you draw cards from the stack, as well as to specify scoring standards.

Spider Solitaire

Spider Solitaire is a more challenging version of the classic solitaire game. The object of the game is to build stacks of same-suit cards in descending order at the same time that you remove cards from the hidden stacks of cards, all with a minimum amount of moves. The scoreboard keeps track of your moves and your points. You can choose from three difficulty levels.

START A WINDOWS XP GAME

You can start all of the Windows XP games in the same manner. Once you launch a game, you can learn more about how to play it by using the Help menu. Some games offer additional options that you can set, such as timing and scoring levels. Others enable you to change the difficulty level. This section shows you how to launch Spider Solitaire, start a new game, and access the Help files.

START A WINDOWS XP GAME

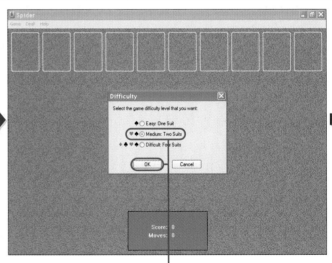

START A GAME

1 Click **Start**.

2 Click **All Programs**.

3 Click **Games**.

4 Click the game you want to play.

SET DIFFICULTY LEVELS

■ The game window appears.

■ This example uses Spider Solitaire.

■ The Difficulty dialog box appears.

5 Click a difficulty level (○ changes to ◉).

6 Click **OK**.

Where can I find other computer games?

Once you start playing the bundled games that come with Windows XP, you may want to try some of the more graphically advanced and challenging games. You can find games and gaming information on the Web, in magazines, and in electronics stores. Before you go shopping, read some Web reviews for computer games to learn more about them. Sites such as Games Domain (www.gamesdomain.com) and Game Spot (www.gamespot.com) offer gaming advice, tips, and user reviews. With so many games to choose from, it is a good idea to do a little research to find the games that are right for you.

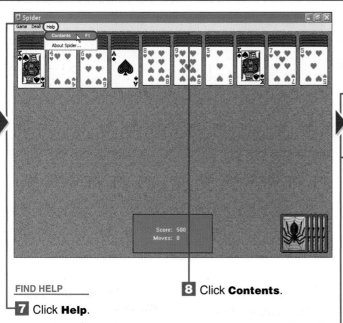

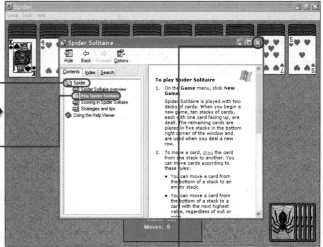

FIND HELP

7 Click **Help**.

8 Click **Contents**.

■ The Help window appears.

9 Click a topic that interests you.

10 Click a subtopic to view the game rules.

11 Click ⊠ to close the Help window.

■ You can now start playing the game.

PLAY A MULTIPLAYER GAME

The Windows XP game bundle includes five Internet games that you can play. Internet games are games that you play with others who log into the Internet at the same time. Not only can you play with other users, but you can also chat with them by typing in your conversations.

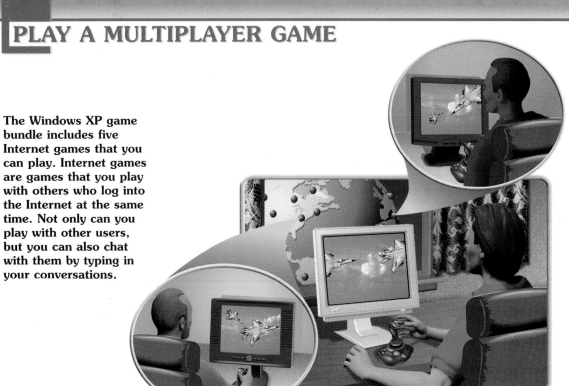

PLAY A MULTIPLAYER GAME

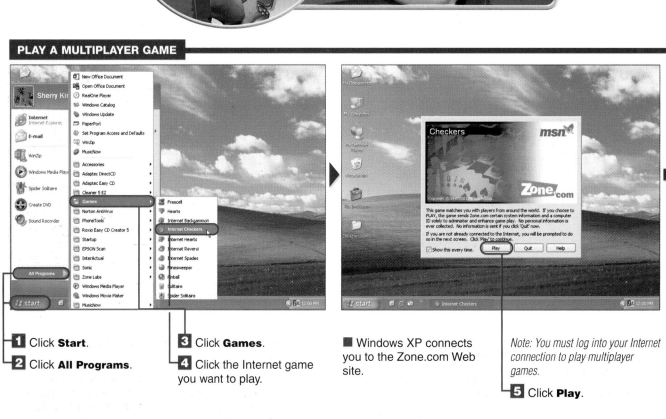

1 Click **Start**.

2 Click **All Programs**.

3 Click **Games**.

4 Click the Internet game you want to play.

■ Windows XP connects you to the Zone.com Web site.

Note: You must log into your Internet connection to play multiplayer games.

5 Click **Play**.

Does Microsoft offer more games that I can install and play with multiple players?

Yes. The Windows XP Extras Web page offers information about the latest games for kids and adults. The site is updated regularly and offers trial versions that you can sample, add-ons, and bonus levels for games. The Windows XP Games page offers a game advisory that you can use to help you determine which games are right for you and your family, and offers a free game download each week. Visit www.microsoft.com/windowsxp/games to access both of these pages.

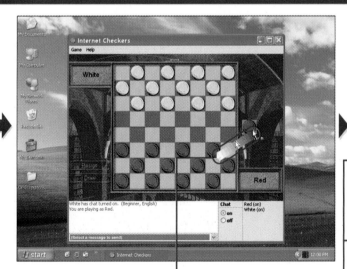

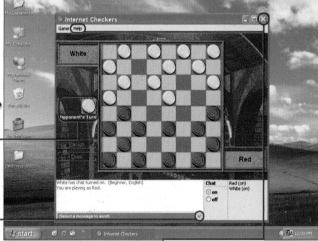

■ The Zone.com server attempts to set you up with other interested players.

■ The game window appears.

■ This example uses the Internet Checkers game.

■ Follow the instructions for play.

6 Click and drag a checker to make a move when it is your turn.

■ Your opponent's turn is indicated here.

■ You can chat with your opponent using this ⌄ and select from conversational phrases that post at the bottom of the window.

7 To exit the game, click ☒.

■ To learn more about playing the game, click the **Help** menu and read the online instructions.

INDEX

INDEX